Nationalism,
Self-Determina[
and the
Quebec Question

Nationalism, Self-Determination and the Quebec Question

DAVID CAMERON

Canadian Controversies Series

Macmillan of Canada / 1974

ISBN   0-7705-0970-3 Cloth
        0-7705-0971-1 Paper

Library of Congress Catalogue Card No.   73-92681

Printed in Canada

TO MY MOTHER
AND THE MEMORY OF
MY FATHER

Contents

Canadian Controversies Series

Canadian political commentators have adopted the full range of political styles, from cold detachment to partisan advocacy. The Canadian Controversies Series is disciplined by the idea that while political analysis must be based on sound descriptive and explanatory modes of thought, social scientists should not abnegate the role of evaluating political systems. Such evaluations require a conscious approach to the interrelationships between facts and values, empirical and normative considerations in politics.

Each theme in the series has been chosen to illustrate some basic principles of Canadian political life and to allow the respective authors freedom to develop normative positions on the related problems. It is hoped that the volumes will stimulate debate and advance public understanding of some of the major questions which confront the Canadian political system. By treating the enduring themes and problems in Canada, the authors will also illustrate the important contribution that social science can offer to politics in terms of facts, ideas, theories and comparative frameworks within which meaningful controversy can take place. Creative political thought must not be divorced from the political fabric of a country but form an integral part of it.

ROBERT J. JACKSON,
General Editor

Preface

Anyone, I suspect, who writes a short book on a large topic is more conscious of what he has left out than what he has put in. This is certainly true in my own case, and I beg the reader's indulgence if he finds, as he almost certainly will, that a favourite nationalist theme or writer or event has been neglected. I have selected for study one of the myriad topics which compose the field of nationalism and as I wrote I have had in mind the English-Canadian reader who is seeking to find his way through the tangles of nationalism and to formulate for himself a satisfactory approach to the issue as it manifests itself in the relations between Quebec and the rest of Canada. There are obviously other worthwhile lines of enquiry that can be and have been pursued, but the one I have adopted has not, so far as I know, been employed in Canada as yet, and it promised to yield fruitful results.

A description of the approach which is taken in this enquiry is provided in the Introduction and need not be repeated here. Perhaps the only point which needs emphasis is the fact that one of the main objectives has been to situate Quebec nationalism in a broader historical and theoretical context; this work is carried out primarily in chapters 2 to 6, and in these pages the reader may feel that he has moved some distance away from nationalism in Canada. But I trust that the justification for the inclusion of this material and the coherence of the argument as a whole will become clear as the study proceeds.

With the stunning victory of the Liberal party in the October 1973 Quebec provincial election, Canadians have been granted a reprieve, at least so far as the confronting of French-Canadian nationalism in its starkest form of *indépendantisme* is concerned. But the contemporary upsurge of nationalism in Quebec has been underway for more than a decade, and it is doubtful that it has yet run its course. Quebec continues to be in the throes of rapid social and economic change, and French Canadians are acutely self-conscious about their collective character and destiny. To me it seems clear that the inevitable medium for the expression of many of Quebec's most significant griev-ances and aspirations will be nationalism, and that Canadians can look ahead to a protracted period of tension and change as the two cultural communities seek to discover a new equilib-rium. A more recent but potentially important phenomenon is the reawakening of consciousness and reflection among English Canadians concerning the shape and values of Canadian society, the bonds which connect the regions and provinces together, and the position of the country in the world. This is certain to complicate French-English relations still further; it may also open up avenues which could not in the past be seriously ex-plored. If the future is murky and obscure, it is as well to be clear about the past and to be critical about the theoretical assumptions and historical beliefs which support and in some measure define human choice. It is as a contribution towards the completion of this difficult task of intellectual clarification that this book is conceived.

While the failings of the book are mine alone, it has been much improved by the comments and assistance of several people, and I am happy to express my appreciation here. Two members of the History Department at Trent, Christopher Greene and Deryck Schreuder, were kind enough to read the bulk of the manuscript and to raise uncomfortable questions, and I am very grateful to them for their help. Armand de Mestral and my colleague, Margaret Doxey, provided some indispensable guidance in chapter 6, and Donald Smiley's com-ments and his trenchant criticism of the manuscript were very much appreciated, even when they were discomfiting. In Diane Mew I was lucky to have an ideal editor, one whose tact, patience and editorial judgment made working with her a great pleasure.

I should like to thank the *Journal of Canadian Studies* for permission to use in chapter 9 some material which appeared in the February 1972 issue of that publication.

This study grew out of a minor disagreement of opinion between myself and Bill Neville, and I should like to take this opportunity to record here my sense of good fortune in having his friendship, and my debt to him, not only for his specific comments on the manuscript, but for the years of intellectual association from which I have derived such benefit while we have been colleagues at Trent.

DAVID CAMERON
Keene, Ontario
April 1974.

1.   Introduction

Of the making of books on nationalism there is no end. This is a book on nationalism and on Canada, but it is, I hope, a book with a difference. Its organizing principle is the concept of national self-determination which provides a fascinating vantage-point from which to view a good deal of what is most significant in the course of public events in contemporary Canada. The idea of national self-determination, while it is especially relevant to Canada today, extends beyond it in a number of different ways, and in order to grasp its significance we must pursue its fortunes beyond the frontiers of this country.

The concept itself has enjoyed a brief but flamboyant career on the world stage. Like nationalism, of which it is a constituent element, it can be seen to have had in eighteenth-century Europe an identifiable beginning, but as yet no end. Its course can be charted in political philosophy, in international law and diplomacy, and in the language of those who seek to advance or to thwart specific nationalist movements. The empirical phenomena to which these notions relate are, of course, everywhere. Nations, national liberation movements, regional languages, ethnic minorities, post-colonial "developing societies"—all these phenomena exist abundantly in the world, and their spokesmen possess in the vocabulary of nationalism a potent political resource. Indeed, so irresistible is the doctrine that we have the curious third-world phenomenon of nationalist movements whose purpose is to promote the interests of nations which by virtually every realistic indicator do not yet exist.

Many commentators express surprise at the continuing strength of nationalism in the twentieth century. A number of the major formal political theories which have permeated the modern world, such as liberal democracy, socialism, and communism, are international and universal rather than national in character and aspiration; and with every major advance in one or another of these doctrines there has been an assumption that the strength of nationalist sentiment would recede. In fact, nothing of the kind has happened. So powerful has been the commitment of people to their own region, their own language, their cultural and historical traditions, and so vigorous their hostility to the domination or control of their community by others, that the competing political theories, in order to achieve worldly success, have been constrained to make an expedient liaison with nationalism, a liaison which is in most cases unsanctified by their own values. Nationalism may not be the most sublime of modern political doctrines but, on the evidence, it is certainly one of the most powerful.

At the level of political theory, it is possible to say that there is a certain conceptual affinity between nationalism and a doctrine such as conservatism.[1] This is significant because one of the most arresting features of conservative thought has been its inability to construct a comprehensive, systematic intellectual framework for itself. A systematic conservative political theory is in a sense impossible, for in the eyes of conservatives such an enterprise would involve the misconceived attempt to articulate a set of interrelated abstract propositions to describe concrete and thoroughly individual situations. If what is important is to be found in the detail, how can one usefully generalize? One cannot *assert* and explain a tradition without altering it; one can only live it.[2] A similar difficulty may exist with respect to nationalism, for it is a doctrine which seeks to describe and justify in general terms the impulse of distinct communities to develop their peculiar genius. Just as a conservative or a traditionalist almost always writes as a member of a particular community facing particular issues and referring to a distinctive historical experience, so a nationalist will carry on his thinking within the context of his own nation and with its problems in mind. It is possible for liberals and socialists to see themselves as citizens of the world and to perceive trans-national bonds superior in importance to the ties of nationality; this is not so easy for nationalists and conservatives, both of whom repose their faith and loyalty in the distinct communities to which they belong.

For more than two centuries the main features of modern

society have been unfolding with ever greater clarity. The signs are everywhere: in the revolution in technology and communications, in industrial economic production, in the increasing size and complexity of organizations, in the acceleration of the pace of change, in the bureaucratization and depersonalization of social functions; even the five, six and seven syllable words we use (as in this sentence above) to describe aspects of our social life themselves reflect the complicated, impersonal world which modern man inhabits.

Significantly, it was at the beginning of this period of historical development that the doctrine of nationalism, with its affirmation of the importance of what is local and idiosyncratic about persons and groups, first appeared in coherent form; and the doctrine has not been far from the centre of political events ever since. Nationalism and nationalist sentiment have sometimes been directly asserted and supported by political leaders, sometimes denied or downgraded in favour of other doctrines, but they are called forth everywhere in periods of crisis. With a sure sense of what would make the strongest appeal, it was "Mother Russia" and not the "Soviet Union" that the communist leaders of the USSR called upon their people to defend during the Nazi invasion. So cheek by jowl with the universal and rational pretensions of the modern world is nationalism; it is difficult to believe that the two phenomena are unrelated, and hard to resist the hypothesis that for modern man each side possesses something which the other side lacks. People who are citizens of the world in aspiration may experience a painful need to belong to a familiar community in actual fact. And not the least important of the many paradoxes of nationalism is the point that in the modern world what is local and non-rational has to be enunciated in universal and rational terms, and the primeval, unspoken bonds of affinity must be transformed into a doctrine.

We shall look at some of these matters in more detail in the pages that follow, but it should be pointed out that it is not our intention to engage in an exhaustive or systematic treatment of nationalism and self-determination as ideas or as political facts. It is rather to provide a theoretical and historical context within which the Canadian experience can be comprehended and assessed. Many aspects of the problems which we as Canadians are currently attempting to face are peculiarly our own, and a knowledge of the detail, the *differentiae* of our situation is indispensable. But at the same time our problems may be understood to have their origins or their counterparts in other times and other places. It is an account of this broader historical, theoretical and cultural context, which is too often neglected by Canadians, that we wish to incorporate into this study.

In Canada, as in many other western countries, the institutions of liberal democracy often fail to satisfy or are in positive conflict with the needs and aspirations of a multinational or multicultural society. Political democracy in western societies, generally speaking, means rule by the majority or, more accurately, rule by representatives chosen by the majority. In circumstances in which the most important political decisions habitually involve cleavage along cultural lines, majority rule in the eyes of the cultural minority can begin to look like a recipe for tyranny and oppression rather than an instrument of self-government. This is why French Canadians speak of "two majorities" in Canadian society, and it is one reason why federalism has proven to be such a popular (and such a fragile) form of government in the modern world.

In Canada political democracy typically does not even mean rule by representatives chosen by the majority; more often than not, our representatives are elected by a large minority of the voters rather than by an actual majority. As an example, with the single exception of the Diefenbaker sweep of 1958, no general election in Canada since the Second World War has produced a government which is based on a majority of the popular vote. This is in fact the normal situation, and is reproduced in provincial and municipal elections all across the country.

Most of us accept or ignore the peculiar arithmetic of political democracy, although in times of crisis when the stakes in an electoral contest are high, the willingness to tolerate these peculiarities drastically diminishes. The most recent examples of just this situation in Canada were the April 1970 and the October 1973 provincial elections in Quebec. In 1970 the Liberals with less than half the popular vote received almost three-quarters of the seats in the National Assembly while the Parti Québécois with almost a quarter of the popular vote got just 6 per cent of the seats. In the 1973 election the disparity between popular votes and seats was even greater, and we shall discuss this matter more fully in Chapter 8. In a sense, these results are not very much more startling than the fact that in the 1972 federal election the Conservative party attracted almost 18 per cent of the popular vote in Quebec, but received not quite 3 per cent of the province's seats. The Conservatives consistently receive about 20 per cent of the popular vote in Quebec and yet in the last four federal elections they have never got more than about 10 per cent of the provincial representation in the House of Commons.

The bias in the voting system against the federal Conservatives in Quebec, which is almost as flagrant as the bias against the PQ, is simply not perceived to be a significant political issue, not even by Robert Stanfield. This is because Mr. Stanfield and others accept the conventions of parliamentary democracy and are prepared to play by the rules of the game as they presently exist; after all, the Conservatives know the system works in their favour elsewhere in the country. Such matters as the system of representation become important political issues when liberal-democratic institutions are subjected to unusual stress, when for some of the participants it becomes more and more difficult to view politics as a game which is played according to certain rules, rather than as a struggle which is carried on in deadly earnest and which is warped in favour of one segment of the society.

The vigorous expression of nationalism in Quebec and the emergence of a strong independence movement have called into question not only French Canada's relation to the rest of the country, but the adequacy of our political institutions as well. What Canadians are facing is a political force which in its direction and intensity threatens our political order with "system overload"; what I believe we as Canadians ought to be pursuing is a resolution of the problem that is consistent with the political values of freedom, self-government and respect for persons which we espouse. I am suggesting, then, that in the last analysis the question of whether or not Quebec separates is secondary.

Of fundamental importance are the effects that the resolution of this conflict, whatever shape it may take, will have on the people who compose the two communities. It is, then, not simply the matter of whether Quebec goes or stays that calls for the attention of Canadians, but the manner of her going or staying, and the purposes that are to be served by either course of action.

That Canadians will cope with this challenge satisfactorily cannot be too easily assumed, for there are people on all sides of the issue who voice opinions which are surely incompatible with the principles that are said to guide our political life. The October crisis of 1970 has brought home to Canadians the vulnerability of modern societies to urban violence and terrorism and has revealed as well the attenuated or confused commitment of many people, within government and without, to humane and civilized values. There are those in English Canada who have advocated the use of force to keep Quebec in Confederation, and there are nationalists in Quebec who see a "real" (French-Canadian) community behind the existent multilingual, plural society that is contemporary Quebec, thus assigning approximately one-fifth of the population of the province to an ambiguous "resident-foreigner" status, despite the fact that in their civil rights and in many cases in their traditional associations as well this fifth are as fully entitled to unfettered membership in the community as anyone else. Both the English Canadian who advocates or would countenance violence and the French-Canadian nationalist who undermines the position of his fellow citizens are elevating a collective ideal above a concern for the welfare of persons, and both are to be resisted. The English Canadian is prepared to risk civil war and civil oppression to maintain the integrity of the Canadian state, and the French Canadian commits himself to a conception of his national community which excludes what he takes to be alien elements — that is, fellow citizens who for one reason or another do not meet his set of cultural criteria.

The temptation to restrict one's political reflection to the abstract concepts of nation, state and class is great, but in my opinion it is one which should not be indulged. Indispensable and illuminating as intellectual categories of analysis, these concepts are too frequently reified and presumed to be natural and autonomous actors in the political world. If this led merely to error in the classroom or study, it might be cause for no serious alarm; but political ideas are a potent force in the world of social action and history offers ample evidence of happiness sacrificed and bones cracked in the service of mistaken or fragmentary beliefs.

It is, I think, only when one ascends to the level of a general theory that one can discern the steadfast march of history; that one can, for example, perceive the inevitability of the struggle of nations for freedom and independence, and the inevitability of their success. Equally, it is at this level that one is able to grasp the "essence" of a phenomenon without essence, and to uncover, with Lord Acton, Pierre Trudeau, Ramsay Cook and others, the stone of reaction and intolerance which corrupts the fruit of every nationalist movement. Such insights are harder to come by for those who stick closer to the ground, but perhaps this is no bad thing.

For Canadians, faced with an upsurge of nationalism in Quebec, strong and growing regional sentiment elsewhere, and the problems of economic dependence in an increasingly volatile world, the public realm is fraught with complexity and the future is obscure indeed. In such circumstances as these, it becomes increasingly important that a community be in a position to make known to itself the interests which it is collectively pursuing and the values to which it aspires, and also that it be capable of carrying out a hard-headed analysis of its actual situation so that a realistic judgment may be made about the degree and extent to which its objectives may be achieved. This is obviously a mammoth and difficult task and, in a country as diverse and as deeply riven with cleavage as Canada, it may not finally be possible to establish more than a formal or a negative description of what the public interest, the good of the country as a whole, might be. For example, it is possible that completion of this task would lead to the conclusion that in Canada the public interest is composed largely of a desire on the part of each of the distinct parts of the country to remain distinct, and a common recognition that this will be a very difficult thing to do in the shadow of the United States.

This is an issue which we cannot approach directly in a work of this kind, although certain aspects of the question will be taken up as the argument progresses. However, despite the diversity of opinion that undoubtedly exists in the country, it is nevertheless possible to suggest that a vitally important set of beliefs which the vast majority of Canadians, whatever their other opinions, hold in common issues out of a commitment to the political values of freedom and democratic government. Indeed, so long as discussion is restricted to the phrase "freedom and democratic government" alone, one can expect well-nigh universal agreement on the critical significance of the values to which the phrase refers; it is when people begin to specify in detail what they take freedom and democracy to mean that conflict and discord set in. We shall have occasion in the course of this study to look a bit more closely at the various things which people have in mind when they employ these concepts, but at this point it can be indicated that it is in the context of this general commitment that we are examining the doctrine of nationalism and the specific forms it has taken in Quebec.

More particularly, in finding our way through the complexities of nationalism, our abiding preoccupation will be with the well-being of persons. One could not be a democrat without accepting the importance of the individual person in defining and setting about to achieve his own welfare, and it would be difficult to be a Canadian without having some inkling of the central importance of a person's cultural affiliations and collective membership in determining and sustaining his personal identity and happiness. A conception of well-being which was exhausted by the idea of material security and possession would miss much of what is most important in the life of man, and within Canada to neglect the importance of either the individual's personal autonomy or his reliance on cultural association for the good life would be to misconstrue the animating spirit of a great many Canadians.

These remarks are of necessity very general, but they indicate nevertheless the perspective from which events in Canada will be viewed; they also underline the obvious but often neglected fact that a country's political institutions exist to serve the needs and interests of its people, and that communities sometimes outgrow the ones that have served them well in the past. Where this can be established, it is foolish to leave such outdated institutions untouched; none other than Edmund Burke puts the case graphically in a speech on economy in government: "when the reason of old establishments is gone, it is absurd to preserve nothing but the burthen of them. This is superstitiously to embalm a carcass not worth an ounce of the gums that are used to preserve it."[3]

Whether we are approaching such a state in the case of Canadian federalism I cannot say, although I would argue that the judgment on this point should be reached, not in the cloisters of academe, nor as a result of an abstract calculation of forces and doctrines, but in the gradually developing opinion of the Canadian people. The authoritative judgment about the serviceability of political institutions should lie with the people who are ostensibly being served by them. In this enterprise the role of political leadership, it seems to me, ought to be akin to that of a midwife assisting in the emergence within Canadian society of some settled view of the situation. This clearly is not an easy task, and unfortunately too often the apparent effect of the activity and statements of public figures is to mystify and obfuscate, to inflame passions which have little hope of being satisfied, rather than to encourage careful reflection about cause and consequence in Canadian public affairs.

This, then, is the general approach we propose to take in our study. Our first task is to clarify certain historical and theoretical issues relating to nationalism.

NOTES

1. This is true despite the fact that nationalism very often acts as a solvent of tradition, whereas conservatism almost always seeks to maintain it.
2. A subtle elaboration of this point can be found in J.H. Levenson's *Confucian China and Its Modern Fate: The Problem of Intellectual Continuity*, 3 vols. (London: Routledge and Kegan Paul, 1958).
3. *The Works of Edmund Burke* (London: George Bell and Sons, 1901), vol. II, p. 83.

2.   Words and Concepts

One of the follies to which students of politics are prone is the insistence upon a greater degree of precision and clarity of definition than the matter under study warrants; to require that a shadow have a sharp outline is to misunderstand what a shadow is.[1] It is often pedantry or an uncontrolled impulse to analyse which subjects general political terms to the unremitting glare of academic scrutiny in the laudable but misplaced effort to uncover their essence. Many terms are best understood in the light of their "use value"; that is to say, in light of the way in which they are employed by people engaged in political activity and the way in which they can be most helpful to those who are thinking and writing about political matters. Clarity is indispensable, of course, but it is primarily a clarity as to the *use* to which a term is being put or will be put, rather than a clarity as to what its *essential meaning* is.

This general issue arises in acute form in the case of the term "nationalism." Clearly, the phenomenon to which this term refers is no shadow; not even in the realm of make-believe could the effects of a shadow be as dramatic as the effects of nationalism have been in the modern world. The difficulty lies rather in the fact that upon inspection "nationalism" turns out to be a term which is customarily applied, not to a single thing, but to a complex set of ideas, attitudes, events and political movements and that these can be related to one another in a virtually infinite variety of ways. In ordinary political discussion we imply a rough-and-ready conception of nationalism and we make rough-and-ready distinctions between nationalism and other closely related phenomena. Common usage can be a helpful guide in our effort to arrive at an illuminating and realistic conception of nationalism; indeed, it may be that what we need at bottom is a clarification and formalization of everyday language.

Starting from this point, it is fair to assume that either too narrow or too all-inclusive a conception of nationalism will not be satisfactory and will not serve our purposes. A restricted view which sees, for example, nationalism as a European phenomenon not only in origin but in continuing fact, which characterizes it solely in linguistic, cultural and traditional-historical terms, and which therefore views the anti-colonial "national liberation" movements of Asia and Africa as nationalist only in an imprecise and misleading sense — this narrow view will not be adequate to our purposes. On the other hand, a view which discovers evidence of nationalism in virtually every expression of group feeling of whatever kind and traces the story of nationalism back into the remote and misty past is far too broad and will not do either.

Unless a person is asked directly to define a word, his understanding of what it means will emerge implicitly and in bits and pieces on the occasions when he uses the word and, equally important, on the occasions when he does not, but selects instead a different but closely related term. No one would use "racism" and "nationalism" interchangeably, although in certain circumstances there may be a considerable overlap in meaning; the sense and connotation of "patriot" and "nationalist" are quite different; and, even when "nation" is being used as a synonym for "state" or "country," it is often possible to discern a subtle principle of selection at work in the way in which people choose between the three terms in particular circumstances. We shall have gone some distance in clarifying our thinking if we can determine the reasons why these and other words differ from one another in ordinary speech.

A common approach to this matter is to examine the origin and history of the relevant words, and it is generally pointed out in books on nationalism that "nation" is derived from a Latin root having to do with birth. This, of course, gives one a hint about certain features of nationalism: for example, that the ties of nationality are commonly related to ancestry and upon occasion rival in strength the immediate ties of blood and kinship in the family. But this approach cannot be much more than suggestive; it provides, for example, no means of discriminating between patriots and patriotism on the one hand and nationalists and nationalism on the other, particularly when one considers that the former terms spring from Greek and Latin roots having to do with fatherhood. Devotion to the land of one's birth and devotion to the land of one's father are not ideas which can be usefully kept apart. That this is more than a mere linguistic quibble can be seen by the fact noted above that we do unconsciously distinguish in our ordinary language between patriotism and nationalism. We shall argue below that the distinction there implied is useful and worth sustaining, despite the fact that it would appear to be obscured rather than clarified by etymological investigation.

There is a large number of expressions which denote a group of people living together in a particular territory: neighbourhood, tribe, clan, province, state, empire and so on. The meanings which have been attached to these terms have frequently changed considerably in history, and words which are virtually synonymous at one point in time break apart and become readily distinguishable at another. The distinction between the terms is generally drawn with reference to the size, type of attachment, and degree of organization of the population to which they refer. "Nation," of course, is another of these words, and the use to which it has been put has altered considerably with the centuries. An example of a distinctive pre-modern usage which is often cited is the division of many medieval universities into "nations," that is, sections representing the regions from which the students have come; the University of Paris was made up of the nations of Picardy, Normandy, France and Germany.

However, an examination of the pre-modern usages of "nation" and related words is at best of limited assistance in the attempt to understand nationalism. This is because nationalism is a modern phenomenon, and prior to its appearance on the historical scene the word and its derivatives were without the connotations and significance they have gradually come to have. Dr. Johnson, in his famous *Dictionary* published in 1755, provides definitions for "nation," "national," "nationally" and "nationalness," but significantly there are no entries at all for "nationalism" or "nationalist." "Nation" is resonant with the ideology of nationalism to modern ears; it was not laden with nationalist associations for our forebears. They did not have in their mind's eye national liberation movements, nation-building, charismatic nationalist leaders and the like. But we do.

Perhaps the most instructive point to note in this respect is the way in which such a word as "nation," for most of its career a serviceable and innocuous term, can be at some point carried to the front lines of history and charged with political dynamite. The appearance of nationalism as a force to be reckoned (and conjured) with was what effected this transformation, and it was the main instrument for shaping and hardening the usage of the word into a few conventional meanings. "Nation" in the cultural or sociological sense came to signify the thing with which nationalists were concerned. A similar, but less enviable fate was in store for the word "race"; racism has to a great extent condemned "race" to an ambiguous nether world in our social and political vocabulary.[2]

Let us consider now what kind of phenomenon nationalists have in mind when they speak of a nation. It will be useful to approach this subject by way of a distinction which Jean-Jacques Rousseau makes in *The Social Contract* (I, v) between an *aggregation* and an *association*. An aggregation for Rousseau is a mere collection of private individuals which is held together by no principle (except force, in certain cases) and which cannot be characterized by any enduring relationships. A throng of people at a fair, a mob, a crowd watching a fire, the passengers and crew of a hijacked airplane are all examples of the sort of thing that Rousseau had in mind when he spoke of an aggregation. An association for Rousseau is quite a different matter. It is a collection of people which has some corporate identity; that is to say, it has some definable purpose or functions, some distinct relationships which characterize its membership, and some enduring existence in time. It may have offices or positions which members from time to time might be expected to fill, or less formally it may have "roles" which various members "play" in the activity of the association. Unlike an aggregation, an association might metaphorically be said to have a life of its own. A bridge club or quilting society, a family, a church, a tribe, a nation, a state are all examples of what Rousseau means by "association."

It can be seen immediately that the things which may

properly be described as associations make up a large and very mixed bag indeed. In pushing our enquiries a step further, let us consider for a moment the commonplace distinction between voluntary associations and associations in which membership is in some sense involuntary. If we look at the examples of a political party and a family the distinction becomes immediately clear. A voluntary association such as a political party is something which a person *chooses* to belong to or not; he takes out a membership and joins the Conservative party or the NDP, and it may be that he resigns his membership if his interest flags or if the party in his opinion does something evil or foolish. Very clearly, a person's relationship to such an organization is voluntary.

But consider the example of a family. This is emphatically not a voluntary association. A person is born into a family and though we might wish it otherwise, birth is not a matter of choice. And just as birth into a family is involuntary, so resignation from a family is impossible. One cannot rationally deny the existence of one's origins and ancestors, although one may certainly deny their relevance. In families there are black sheep, but whatever their actions and however acute the discomfort which they wreak on their suffering kin, they still remain members of the family.

In these two examples the distinction between voluntary and involuntary associations is dramatic; but in many instances it is quite seriously blurred, and it becomes necessary to think of the categorization of voluntary and involuntary associations as a continuum rather than as a description of polar opposites. We mentioned above as an example of a voluntary association the political party, and we had in mind the kind of organization one finds in a western multiparty system. But what about the political party in a single-party state? In many countries there is just one official political party and all others are banned. In such circumstances, where membership in the party is a virtual precondition to lawful political activity of any kind, the extent to which it can be reasonably termed a voluntary association is called very much into question. A similar situation exists in the case of many trade unions. If a person working at a particular job is genuinely free to join the union or not, then it is fair to characterize the union as a voluntary association. But if the person is working in a closed-shop situation, and cannot continue in his employment if he does not join the trade union, then his membership in that association cannot be reasonably considered purely voluntary.

A case in point which is closer to our present concerns is the state, which exhibits to a striking degree the mixture of volition and necessity that can characterize human associations. We are all born into some political jurisdiction, and are raised as Canadian or French or German citizens (or potential citizens) whether we like it or not. In this respect, then, being the subject of a specific sovereign authority is in no sense a matter of choice; we take our lumps in much the same way that we do in the case of the family.

Nevertheless, while state membership can be seen to be involuntary in the sense specified above, it involves an element of choice in most cases as well. Some political theorists have even gone so far as to suggest a formal contractual agreement which an individual would make when he reaches maturity; in such an agreement, a person would pledge his allegiance to the state and enter into the rights and obligations of full citizenship. This is certainly not common practice in fact, but something very like this takes place when immigrants to a country are naturalized; they are granted citizenship, usually after a provisional period of residence, and upon fulfilling the necessary requirements and declaring their commitment to their adopted country. It is evident from this example that, subject to certain controls and restrictions and assuming that the right of emigration is recognized by one's native land, it is possible for a person to break his ties with one country and assume a new legal attachment to another. What is not really possible today — and this is one of the things that sets state membership off from a host of subordinate associations — is the rejection of or the escape from all political jurisdictions whatsoever. One may be able to choose within limits *which* state one wishes to be associated with, but one cannot choose *whether* one wishes to be associated with any state at all.

In the eighteenth century Samuel Johnson gave the following definition of "nation": "a people distinguished from another people, generally by their language, original, or government." This is economical but ambiguous, for it covers over the two dominant usages of the term and its derivatives in English. The first usage might be named *juridical* in which the term is employed as a synonym for "state," as in "The United Nations," "the national debt" or "international relations" — in Johnson's definition, "a people distinguished by their government." One of the reasons for its widespread employment in English in this way may be the absence of a satisfactory adjective for "state." To speak of a nation in this juridical sense is to speak of a country in its political and legal aspect; that is to say, as the possessor of sovereign power, an established government, with the right in international affairs to represent and speak for its people — in a word, as a state.

The second usage is *sociological;* that is to say, the term "nation" is employed to indicate a large group of people who have some principle of unity and identity other than, or in addition to, simple common membership in a state. The precise character of the relationship—be it linguistic, historical or "aspirational"—may vary a good deal, but it is of the essence of the sociological conception of the nation that it be extra-political. Apart from anything else, it must be if it is to do the work that it is often expected to do. For example, when people speak of a right of national self-determination they are not usually referring to the autonomy of states; rather, they are referring to the right of distinct groups of people to decide for themselves what social and political structures they will live under. The stated objective in such a discussion may be and often is the creation of a sovereign power, a state, but the assumption necessarily is that the community does not yet possess sovereign independence. When we speak of Canada as a member of the Commonwealth of Nations we are using the juridical meaning; when we speak of French Canada as a nation we are using the sociological meaning. Needless to say, our primary concern in this study is with the sociological conception of the nation.

Where does the nation in this latter sense fit in Rosseau's categorization of social groups as aggregations or associations? Clearly, a nation is an association, for an essential part of the conception of a nation is that it has a corporate identity and an existence in time and that its members may be identified by certain common characteristics. Even in the case where it is a question of "building a nation" (an idea which we shall have occasion to consider subsequently), there is an assumed unity of aspiration and a collective will which identify and mark off the population in question. The sociological conception of a nation presupposes that it is possible to comprehend the nation as an organized structure even in the absence of legal or juridical incorporation. A state does not exist in the absence of political and legal definition (such as sovereign authority in its jurisdiction, the ability to establish and maintain civil order, legislative, executive and judicial institutions, formal recognition by other sovereign powers, and so on); a nation, however, can and often does exist in the absence of such definition, for its identity is not finally dependent on political, but on extra-political factors.

As to the question of whether the nation is better understood as a voluntary or non-voluntary association, the formal position is reasonably clear. For the limited purposes of discussion let us say that a nation is a substantial body of people who have, and see themselves as having, some significant things in common beyond bare membership in a political order, and for whom that fact is of significant political relevance. Obviously, this is a loose and incomplete characterization but it does bring out two points.

In the first place, where there is a nation one can expect to find in it objective characteristics which set that group off from the others around it: language, custom and tradition, memory of a collective past, religious belief, racial affinity— these are the classic characteristics by which a nation is defined. It is generally possible for a neutral observer to identify a number of features of this kind which bind a group together and distinguish it from adjacent populations. The possession of national political institutions has, of course, very often been a factor of vital importance in creating and sustaining national identity, but it is essential to the sociological conception of the nation that national identity can be understood exclusive of the possession of these institutions. In the second place, where there is a nation one can expect to find among its members a consciousness of this fact; that is to say, the group will not only be characterized by certain empirically observable characteristics, but also by a collective self-consciousness. Individuals see themselves as members of a nation, as having a national as well as a personal identity.

There is, then, both an objective and a subjective component in the constitution of a nation. But, certainly in the case of the European nations, it is fair to say that the subjective component is derivative. Individuals are conscious of membership in a nation by virtue of the fact that there are certain significant characteristics which they share with others of the same nationality; self-consciousness rests upon the actual ties and affinities of nationality. All of which is to suggest that a nation is a form of association which is typically to be found towards the non-voluntary end of the continuum. It bears some resemblance to the family as an association (consider the roots of the words "nation" and the French "patrie") and, rather like the family, it may plausibly be regarded as a "natural" association; certainly this is an important assumption in much nationalist theory.

An example will bring these points into bolder relief. Great Britain is composed of four major nationalities: the English, Scottish, Welsh and Irish. Although people talk of Great Britain as a nation-state, that is, a state composed of a single nation, this usage is either imprecise or describes a fact (the British nation) which is still very much in the making. If this is true of Great Britain, one of the most frequently cited examples of a nation-state, then we can assume it applies to other nation-states as well. Each of Britain's national groups is marked by many of the classic characteristics of a nation and each has been conscious over a great many years of its distinctive identity. Today, as one would expect, the dominant national group, the English, are the least conscious of themselves as a distinctive entity, but with the existence of small, but significant, nationalist and secessionist groups in Scotland and Wales and the continuing problems of a divided Ireland, there can be no doubt that the other three groups are conscious, often painfully conscious, of their identity and collective position in the social and political affairs of Britain.

Now, nations as we have described them above have existed for a very long time, but nationalism has not. One way of characterizing nationalism in terms of our analysis above is to say that it appears when the self-consciousness of the nation turns into a collective expression of *will,* an intention to move in a certain direction, to achieve some specific object of desire. This presupposes some general dissatisfaction with the current condition of the nation, and indeed nationalism typically emerges out of a sense of frustration, thwarted ambition, or collective irritation with the warping or blockage of the natural force of the nation. There will be no nationalism with a nation contented. To use Lord Acton's example of Poland in the eighteenth century, it was the systematic dismemberment of the Polish people that caused the anguish in which nationalist feelings were seeded, and it was the will of the Poles to reconstitute themselves as a single community that led Lord Acton to suggest this case as one of the earliest and perhaps the first coherent expression of nationalism.

It is possible to identify two features of early modern Europe which are of particular significance in the emergence of nationalism, one of them social and the other broadly intellectual. As for the first, nationalism is the product of an age when for the first time in centuries of European history the mass of the population became a factor of crucial importance in the working out of political affairs. Not, perhaps, since classical Greece and republican Rome had there been a widely defined citizen body actively engaged in politics, and even there the definition was not as broad as it might seem at first glance. The Athenian city-state which Pericles so eloquently apostrophized in Thucydides' *History of the Peloponnesian Wars* excluded slaves, resident foreigners and women from the franchise; only a tiny minority of fifth-century Athens enjoyed political rights. In the early modern period there was a successive broadening of the conception of the people, with the result that new classes, new professions and new religious minorities were admitted to the ranks of citizenship. The irrepressible Abbé Sieyès in the eighteenth century put the superficially innocuous question: *Qu'est-ce que le Tiers Etat?*—who composes the Third Estate in France? The political classes in France were divided into the clergy (First Estate), nobility

(Second Estate), and the commons (Third Estate). But to his innocuous question Sieyès provided a revolutionary answer, for in his pamphlet he asserted that the Third Estate is in fact the French nation; those who are not members of it (Sieyès had in mind the privileged classes) are no part of France at all. It is in this atmosphere of popular sovereignty and mass political participation that nationalism first appears and in which it has flourished ever since.

Ideology. The second point is related to the first. The modern political world is not only democratic, at least in aspiration or formal statement, but also decidedly ideological in its approach to politics. There is a deeply felt need in individuals and groups to clothe their actions and their hopes in a general statement of principles or to employ a kind of political metaphysic as a guide to their activity. This has meant that what have come to be called ideologies—that is to say, comprehensive theoretical systems that provide or are taken to provide a framework and a guide to political practice—have been very much in vogue. Many people have noticed the importance of "isms"—liberalism, socialism, communism, fascism—in the modern world, and each of these can be understood as an ideology. Nationalism is such another and, as we have suggested, the most successful of them all.

Elie Kedourie provides a concise summary of the main principles composing the doctrine at the beginning of his book on nationalism. "It pretends," he writes, "to supply a criterion for the determination of the unit of population proper to enjoy a government exclusively its own, for the legitimate exercise of power in the state, and for the right organization of a society of states. Briefly, the doctrine holds that humanity is naturally divided into nations, that nations are known by certain characteristics which can be ascertained, and that the only legitimate type of government is national self-government."[3]

Two things may be noted about this doctrine. First, it is through and through *political* in character. Although one assumption of a nationalist is that he and his fellows will only find personal fulfillment within the confines of the nation, the cutting edge of nationalism appears in the belief that the nation itself can only flourish if it can pursue its destiny untrammelled and unimpeded; what this means in substance is that the nation must constitute itself as a state and enjoy sovereign independence. Second, it has a very clear thrust or direction. It indicates how to view the political world, it identifies the critical political actors (*nations,* not individuals, kings or classes) and, most important, it presupposes throughout the imperfection of contemporary reality. Clearly, the world is not now satisfactorily divided up into sovereign nation-states; if it were nationalist ideology would atrophy and wither away.

Perhaps a word might be said here about the distinction between nationalism and patriotism. The two concepts are often confused and the two terms sometimes used interchangeably, but it is possible and useful to keep them apart. We have suggested above that nationalism is a modern phenomenon, that it arose in an era in which mass political participation and an ideological style of politics became important, and that it is itself the most powerful of modern political ideologies and on the evidence the most effective at moving large populations into action. Patriotism is none of these things. It pre-dates the modern world by centuries, it is in no way dependent upon mass participation in politics, it is not an ideology nor is it necessarily related to politics or to political change. Patriotism is a much more ordinary affair than nationalism, quite without the theoretical pretensions of the latter, and it involves a love of one's native land together with a commitment where necessary to defend it and its interests. Affection is directed not so much to the nation as to the country or homeland, which may be a territory in which a variety of ethnic groups co-exist. A Swiss can be a patriot; it would be difficult for him to be a Swiss nationalist. It is obvious that the ideas are closely related at many points, but we are attempting here to uncover the differences which are often hinted at in everyday speech and which clarity of thought bids us retain.

We mentioned above the paradox of a strong nationalist movement existing despite (or perhaps because of) the apparent absence of a nation. This phenomenon has characterized the countries of the so-called third world and in particular has marked the wave of nationalism that swept through the European overseas colonies after the Second World War, leading to vigorous national liberation movements and ultimately, in most cases, to independence.

From the point of view of the student of nationalism who comes to this phenomenon with European models in mind, there are bound to be difficulties with this "nation-less" breed of nationalism. A typical situation, for example, in Africa, is one in which a European country towards the end of the last century establishes for itself a colonial territory in a region which has not hitherto experienced this type of administration. The boundary and organization of the territory are determined by the fortunes of conquest, by rivalry with competing imperial powers, and by the needs of European-style military and public administration. The obscure but important traditional boundaries of the indigenous cultures are ignored and submerged. When the drive for independence comes, it is on behalf of this European-defined territory that the adherents struggle. The population of this territory may be extraordinarily diverse, with a wide variety of languages, cultures and tribal affiliations and with a history of internecine struggles rather than the unifying experience of common enterprise. By any of these indicators, then, it is the reverse of a national community, and yet it is said that this population is engaged in a struggle for national independence. Why? It can, I think, be established that it is intelligible and appropriate to understand such cases (and there are many of this type) as instances of nationalism; but the thing is shot through with ironies, and it is important to appreciate the grounds for viewing them in this light.

What at bottom unites and defines this diverse population is a common sense of oppression by a specific imperial power. One irony is that the people are constituted by that very foreign power which subsequently comes under attack, but it is the fact itself which sets in motion the course of events which leads the population to conceive of themselves as a distinct people and potentially as a nation. Nationalism was not simply imported to these lands by native intellectuals who had picked up European ideas in their studies at metropolitan universities; it was also in part created by the very fact of colonialism to which it was a direct reaction. This group self-consciousness may develop slowly during the period of colonial rule, but at some point it is transformed into a collective will to shrug off the entanglements and indignities of colonial status and assume the responsibilities of independent self-government. This, then, is the driving force which is characterized as nationalism, and it is defined by a common experience or sense of oppression and a common desire for independence. Its specific political objective is not secession and the creation of a new state or a new territory; it is rather the expulsion of foreign rulers from an existing political jurisdiction and the assumption of power by the indigenous population or its representatives.

Success in achieving this objective is just the beginning for the country concerned, as can be seen in the use of the term "nation-building" and in the invention of the concept of "neo-colonialism." So long as the struggle for independence continues there is a built-in principle of unity: opposition to foreign rule. Once independence is achieved, it becomes necessary to find for the diverse groups that compose the new state a basis of unity more substantial than that summed up in the phrase "my enemy's enemy is my friend." The decolonized countries of the third world have followed two main lines in this connection, and have sometimes pursued both simultaneously. The first and major course of action has been to enlist the population in the all-consuming task of building the nation which they have already liberated. In concrete terms, this generally involves a policy of national economic development and the implementation of a wide range of social policies to increase health and literacy, and to create the technical skills necessary to operate a modernizing economy and to man the expanding bureaucratic structures of an increasingly complex community. The second and often less happy course of action has been to re-invent an enemy which all members of the society can join in opposing—hence neo-colonialism. In many cases, the fears about new patterns of foreign control are not chimerical; Canadians have had sufficient experience of the combination of formal sovereignty and *de facto* dependence to be sensitive to this type of problem. But, to paraphrase Voltaire, if neo-colonialism did not exist, it would have to be invented (and often is), for its use in binding an ex-colonial country together is too obvious to be ignored. And it is apparent that as a device of national integration it does not matter so much whether neo-colonialism is real or not so long as it is believed.

This brief discussion of nationalism in the third world indicates the extraordinarily wide range of the phenomenon in contemporary political affairs and suggests something of its adaptability and appeal. It also brings out a feature of some importance in our general understanding of nationalism. We have remarked on the irony of nationalism without a nation, but in our discussions of this matter we should not lose sight of the dynamic and developmental character of the phenomenon of nationalism. We shall examine this more fully in the sections on self-determination, but it is worth noting at this point that an integral element of nationalist doctrine is the self-transforming, self-constituting potentialities of nations. They are, in a sense, always in the making, and therefore perennially incomplete. The so-called developing nations are engaged in a more dramatic and radical task of self-creation than are many other national communities; they are pulling themselves up by their bootstraps. But it is fair to assume that a similar if more decorous and less exciting process is going on elsewhere, and in that respect there is an affinity between third-world and other kinds of nationalism. The rub comes in the developing countries when there does not seem to be a self to determine; but we will address ourselves more fully to this later. However, let us first turn to a consideration of the early history of nationalism.

NOTES

1. Aristotle puts it nicely: "It is the mark of an educated man to look for precision in each class of things just so far as the nature of the subject admits; it is evidently equally foolish to accept probable reasoning from a mathematician and to demand from a rhetorician scientific proofs." (*Ethics*, I, iii, 1094.)
2. Kenneth Minogue makes this point in *Nationalism* (Baltimore: Penguin Books, 1970), p. 9.
3. *Nationalism* (London: Hutchison University Library, 1961), p.9.

3. The Roots of Nationalism: America, France and Germany

Nationalism, as an articulated set of political beliefs, appeared about the time of the French Revolution. The Revolution in France at the end of the eighteenth century is an event of profound significance in the transformation and development of western political ideas and in the history of nationalism, but it is not at all self-evident what precisely its significance is.

The earlier American Revolution is not problematic in the same sense, even though it was a separatist struggle for independence. It is an event of the first importance in the history of the eighteenth century. It caused a sensation in Europe, and especially in France. It attracted many European political adventurers and idealists to its side; and the homespun philosopher and American revolutionary leader Benjamin Franklin took Paris by storm when he crossed the Atlantic to seek assistance and to represent the interests of the rebelling colonies. America as well became a factor in the continuing struggle between Great Britain and France. The French government was not visibly upset to see its old and resourceful enemy fighting desperately to keep down a rebellion in her own backyard, nor did France scruple to provide aid to the American rebels when that seemed to suit her own interests.

There was never much doubt, either within the colonies or without, about the basis of their conflict with Great Britain, and the emerging American community remained remarkably faithful to the principles and purposes for which it was fighting. For much of their early career, the colonies grew up under the "benign neglect" of the mother country, and the formative influence on their character and institutions was that of the Puritan settlers. What appears to have happened at the outset was the abstraction and purification of one important element in English social and political life, namely, the tradition of individualism, rooted first of all in religious dissent, but rapidly extending into all spheres of life and developed into a general view of society and human affairs.

In politics this tradition of individualism and dissent took the form of liberal and democratic political beliefs, and a firm unwillingness to accept a form of rule perceived to be paternal and not in accord with the dignity of free men. The specific conflict which precipitated armed struggle adequately suggests this fact; the controversy was about whether the British Parliament had a right to tax the colonies in the absence of colonial representation in Parliament. It was within the general framework of political and economic liberalism, then, and it continued to be within these terms, that the Americans fought their war.

It is quite possible retrospectively to impose the vocabulary and concepts of nationalism on the American Revolution, but to do so would be profoundly misleading. It was not perceived in that way by the participants, and in fact it preceded by a generation the full development of a nationalist vocabulary which politicians, publicists and intellectuals could use in their actual political activity. What existed in eighteenth-century America was thirteen distinct social and political entities with a common grievance. The American nation has been formed gradually out of circumstance and political leadership; the Revolution was one of the first steps in this long and painful process. Despite the fact that an American Revolution can only be imperfectly understood as a national liberation movement, the United States of America was, in the words of the American social scientist, Seymour Martin Lipset, the "first new nation," and its successful nation-building effort has provided a model for many similar attempts to follow.

The American Revolution need not, I think, provide a problem of interpretation for the student of nationalism, since it may intelligibly be understood as the culmination or the practical expression of a set of political ideas which are not primarily nationalist in character. The French Revolution, on the other hand, seems best understood as a transitional, and hence irreducibly ambiguous, phenomenon. Of the American Revolution Tom Paine said: "To know whether it be the interest of this continent to be independent, we need only ask this easy, simple question: Is it the interest of a man to be a boy all his life?"[1] Nothing was ever quite as simple as Tom Paine supposed, and it may be noted parenthetically that he generously included all of British North America in his capacious statement; but his rhetorical question with its image of a boy on the threshold of adulthood nevertheless does nicely suggest the optimism, the enthusiasm and the noble aspiration of that period of American history. The French Revolution, on the other hand, is veined with tragedy and defeat, and the images appropriate to it are not those of maturation, but rather those of death and birth, or perhaps birth in death.

At any rate, if one were disposed to look for apparent manifestations of nationalism prior to the 1790s, it would not be to America that one would direct one's attention; a more likely place, following Lord Acton, might be Poland in the 1770s and later. Of the effects of the cynical partitioning of that country by Russia, Austria and Prussia, Acton has written:

> For the first time in modern history a great State was suppressed, and a whole nation divided among its enemies. This famous measure, the most revolutionary act of the old absolutism, awakened the theory of nationality in Europe, converting a dormant right into an aspiration, and a sentiment into a political claim. . . . Thenceforward there was a nation demanding to be united in a State, — a soul, as it were, wandering in search of a body in which to begin life over again; and, for the first time, a cry was heard that the arrangement of States was unjust — that their limits were unnatural, and that a whole people was deprived of its right to constitute an independent community.[2]

Here are the genuine signs of nationalism: the transformation of a dormant right into an aspiration and a sentiment into a political claim; the notion of natural political boundaries; the demand of a historic community to possess its own state. When Acton speaks of a "dormant right" he is implying quite rightly that by the 1770s there had already been a profound shift in European political consciousness, because the right which lay dormant in Poland until it was disturbed and ultimately flouted and denied is quite simply the most fundamental nationalist principle, that is to say, the right of a nation, however defined, to a separate political existence. This was not a principle that had existed in any distinct form for very long in European history, and Acton notes that in the old European system which existed well into the eighteenth century the rights of nations were neither recognized by governments nor asserted by the people: "The interest of the reigning families, not those of the nations, regulated the frontiers."[3] There had long been feelings of patriotism, of love for and commitment to one's own land, but it is when this primordial and often apolitical sentiment is transformed into a political claim, and in consequence undergoes elaboration and sophisticated articulation, that one can look for the appearance of nationalism.

What about the French Revolution? Of its significance there can be no doubt. Edmund Burke recognized immediately that the western world was crossing a historical watershed and almost before the Revolution was properly underway he wrote: "It appears to me as if I were in a great crisis, not of the affairs of France alone, but of all Europe, perhaps of more than Europe. All circumstances taken together, the French Revolution is the most astonishing that has hitherto happened in the world."[4] He was right, and since he penned these words the Revolution has remained by all odds the dominant fact of subsequent French political history and has become the classic revolutionary model for advocates and opponents of radical change everywhere. Its status as a revolution, then, is unimpeachable, and it is an event of an utterly different order from the so-called Glorious Revolution of 1688 in England and, arguably, from the American Revolution as well.

But if it stands as the paradigm case of the type revolution, its character beyond that is very complex and has proved to be extraordinarily difficult to unravel. It has been subjected to protracted and at times violent debate and to the most disparate interpretations. It has been viewed as a bourgeois revolution in which the rising middle class assaulted the barriers of privilege which denied them access to the levers of political power; as a broadly social revolution which engaged the mass of people and involved the upsetting of a wide range of established social and political structures; as a revolution that succeeded and as a revolution that failed; as the culmination of the goals and aspirations of the eighteenth-century movement of ideas called the Enlightenment, and as an abrupt and dramatic rejection of those aspirations; as the first wide-ranging nationalist movement—and, of course, as a host of other things as well.

It would not be surprising if elements of all these things were represented in a series of events that continued for a decade. But, happily, we need not enter the critical fray beyond seeking to assess the French Revolution in the context of our interest in the emergence of nationalism.

One of Edmund Burke's central criticisms of the French revolutionaries is levelled at what he takes to be their doctrinaire adherence to an abstract set of social and political propositions and, still worse, their ignorant attempt to realize these principles in practice. Perhaps more explicitly than anyone else at the time, he connected false theory with corrupt practice and saw the fanatical idealism of the revolutionaries and the single-minded effort to apply an elliptical, fragmentary political theory as a major, if not *the* major cause of the evils to which France was subjected. He speaks of "this barbarous philosophy, which is the offspring of cold hearts and muddy understandings,"[5] and says of its proponents: "Their liberty is not liberal. Their science is presumptuous ignorance. Their humanity is savage and brutal."[6] He even attacks the reorganization of France into new administrative regions as yet another example of the Revolution's foolish application of abstract "reason" to human affairs:

It is boasted that the geometrical policy has been adopted, that all local ideas should be sunk, and that the people should no longer be Gascons, Picards, Bretons, Normans; but Frenchmen, with one country, one heart, and one Assembly. But instead of being all Frenchmen, the greater likelihood is, that the inhabitants of that region will shortly have no country.[7]

For Burke, then, the Revolution is shot through with paradox: reason breeds unreason; science is grounded in ignorance; the pursuit of liberty issues in despotism, the more single-minded the pursuit, the more despotic the result; and the most sublime humanitarian aspirations are perfectly compatible with brutality and degradation.

It seems fair to say that Burke in many important respects misunderstood the upheaval in France, and that in particular his preoccupation with revolutionary ideology led him to minimize the structural rigidities, flagrant injustices and genuine physical hardships which were bedevilling French society. There were, after all, a succession of crop failures and consequent food shortages, an entrenched and virtually immovable aristocracy with privileges vastly incommensurate with its functions, and a weak and ineffectual royal administration. Also, there was throughout the eighteenth century the systematic exclusion of the increasingly important middle class from political activity, and the related separation of those who talked and wrote about politics from those who engaged in it. Indeed, this last may have been a factor of some importance in establishing the gulf between theory and practice and in ushering in the reign of paradox that Burke so much deplores.

Nevertheless, Burke's insight into the ideology of the French Revolution was profound. It helps for a start to explain the vexing ambiguity of events in revolutionary France and the consequent difficulties of interpretation. For if the Revolution was very much a creature of the Enlightenment in aspiration, it was also and undeniably a progenitor of the Romantic era in effect. That it was the first can be seen in many of the public documents of the period, for example, the series of revolutionary constitutions which include the Declaration of the Rights of Man and of the Citizen; that it was the second is exemplified by Wordsworth in his twenties who combined youth, poetry, politics and a continental affair in a paroxysm of revolutionary ardour.

What is particularly helpful in Burke's diagnosis is the demonstration that a theory of politics and political activity that is grounded in false assumptions can result in the opposite of what is expected when it is applied. For it is clear that so far as an articulated political theory was a factor in the course of events in France in the 1790s, it was composed of an extension and an application of Enlightenment political thought; that is to say, it reflected the liberal and in some cases the democratic ideals of earlier writers and saw in the transformation of eighteenth-century France (and the recent appearance on the world scene of the United States of America) the realization and gradual extension of these universally applicable ideals. The view of many participants was that republican France, both in its internal upheavals and in its military ventures in Europe, was engaged in what was potentially a worldwide movement of social and political reform. A new world was in the making.

But it is true as well that, whatever the purity of motivation and the nobility of the goals, the facts very often presented a stark contrast. Even if one makes a generous allowance for the pain and unpredictability of revolutionary change, it must have seemed to contemporaries that Burke had a point, that the pursuit of liberty seemed most often to end up in anarchy or dictatorship, or in a rapid-fire succession of both. Indeed, Hannah Arendt, a modern political theorist, has gone so far as to set the American above the French Revolution on the grounds that the former succeeded in constituting liberty anew, whereas the latter dramatically and demonstrably failed in this enterprise.

It would be foolish to deny that there were elements of nationalist sentiment in revolutionary opinion and that the increasingly coherent conception of the corporate body of the French nation made great strides during this period. The Constituent Assembly, which passed the famous Declaration of Rights in 1789, also passed a decree altering Louis XVI's title from "Louis, by the grace of God, King of France and Navarre" to "Louis, by the grace of God and the constitutional law of the state, King of the French"—*roi des Français*.[8] The change is significant, but ambiguous. It is clear that an increased emphasis is being placed on the population, the people of France as a whole, but what is not clear is whether the people are conceived as such by virtue of their having certain cultural traits in common (such as the French language, shared historical traditions, and so on), or by virtue of their enjoying certain democratic rights and duties as citizens. The phrase in question, *roi des Français*, will of course sustain both interpretations, but it is our contention that it is liberal-democratic and not nationalist beliefs that predominate here.

The meaning of many of the events of the French Revolution are ambiguous in this way, and provide empirical examples of the close historical (but not logical) relationship which obtains between liberal democracy and nationalism and which we shall consider in more detail below. Two specific examples of ambiguity will suffice to demonstrate this point. The first involves military affairs. The ragged and unprofessional armies of republican France astonished Europe with their successes, and people were not slow to remark one of their main distinguishing features; they were citizen armies, called up from the ranks of the population as a whole and led, not by aristocrats with inherited or purchased commissions, but by soldiers who emerged out of the same classes as those they led. This was a far cry from the mercenary and professional forces directed by members of the traditional ruling classes which were typical of European armies at that time. It is easy to view France in this respect as a nation-in-arms depending upon and calling forth nationalist emotions and an aggressive sense of French superiority. But to see it solely from this restricted perspective is inadequate, for republican France was also acting out a drama from the distant past. There was a long tradition of what might be called classical republicanism in political theory which grew out of an admiration for the classical Greek city-states and republican Rome. Rome, Athens and Sparta were influential models during the Enlightenment, and many thinkers believed that one reason for the remarkable military valour of these communities and for the importance which citizenship assumed for them could be found in the practice of raising armies out of the able-bodied citizenry. This theme of a citizen militia and a corresponding hostility to mercenary and professional armies was raised again and again in the early modern period by such writers as Machiavelli, Harrington, Montesquieu and Rousseau, and became an element of some importance in most republican and much liberal political theory. In any appreciation of the ideological significance of the armies of the Revolution this factor, not nationalist but liberal and republican in character, cannot be neglected.

The second example is related. It is clear that Burke was not alone among European statesmen in thinking that revolutionary France had contracted a highly infectious and virulent ideological disease which was in danger of sweeping like a plague across the face of Europe. But what was the nature of the disease? Here we enter upon one of the ironies with which history is strewn. Voltaire said that history is a pack of tricks which the living play on the dead; but history plays tricks on the living as well. Revolutionary France saw itself as having a sacred mission, and we shall have occasion to note subsequently the frequency with which a sense of mission is linked to nationalism; in this case, though, the mission in question was the advancement of civilization and progress in the form of a radical egalitarianism and democratic political institutions. Napoleon, when he was still a young general commanding an army of the Directorate in the invasion of Italy, made the following public declaration:

> Peoples of Italy, the French army comes to break your chains; the French people is the friend of all peoples; meet us with confidence. Your property, your religion, and your usages will be respected. We make war as generous enemies, and we have no quarrel save with the tyrants who enslave you.[9]

The French, at least in their public expressions of intent, were not seeking to subjugate foreign people in a war of nationalist expansion or even to assist other European nations to liberate themselves from foreign domination; they were rather attempting to break the chains which bound people to tyrants, to assist citizens everywhere to take up their democratic rights. The irony is that, although the mission was liberal and democratic, the reaction was nationalist. The French hoped to bring freedom and equality to Europe and tried to encourage people to rise up against their rulers and against the indigenous institutions of privilege; but when people rose up, it was not simply against their rulers, but against French occupation and French aggression as well. In retrospect this does not seem surprising; French motives were mixed, and one cannot neglect old-fashioned *real politik*, with its goals of state security and territorial gain, as a factor of considerable importance in any assessment of the foreign policy of republican France.

The doctrine of revolutionary France was "liberté, égalité et fraternité." The image of a republican France, engaged in fraternal association with its fellow European peoples in shedding the bonds of tyranny, was bound to suffer alteration in the course of a decade of revolution and a generation of bitter international warfare. At the beginning of the period, the *fraternité* which was emblazoned on banners and engraved on the minds of the citizens was fraternity according to the Enlightenment model, not according to the nationalist model. It was the universality of the brotherhood of man, not the exclusivity of the ties of blood and nationality. It must be said, however, that one of the casualties of a generation of domestic and international violence was that very cosmopolitan idealism which had been the animating spirit of the Enlightenment and which had been an important element in the Revolution at its inception.

The European intellectual community greeted the Revolution in France at its outset with fascination and, in a great many cases, with initial approval. Kant, Wordsworth, Coleridge, Goethe and Fichte are merely a few of the more obvious examples of writers in England and Germany who reacted with initial warmth or even enthusiasm to the events in France. To understand why this should be so it is necessary to have some appreciation of the position of France in eighteenth-century Europe.

Throughout the eighteenth century France was unquestionably the social and intellectual leader of Europe, and Paris was for that period the undisputed capital of European civilization. French was the language of culture and diplomacy, and even within the borders of many other European countries French was the language of the upper classes; Frederick the Great was patronizing about the German language, preferred to speak French, and did his best to keep abreast of intellectual happenings in Paris. Even after the French Revolution and the traumatic experience of the Napoleonic invasions, Frederick William II of Prussia could speak German only with difficulty and the German patriot Stein customarily used French with his family.[10] So it was to Paris that ambitious writers and artists flocked and it was in the grand salons of the French capital that the aristocratic and intellectual worlds of the continent met and commingled.

Earlier we remarked on the fact that a deep gulf existed between the intellectual and cultural life of France on the one hand and government and practical political activity on the other. It was, of course, the first which occasioned the admiration and emulation of Europe; Frederick the Great was a great admirer of French civilization—he was no lover of French foreign policy. K. R. Minogue notes that for roughly half the eighteenth century, while British and French intellectuals such as Voltaire, Montesquieu, Hume, Rousseau and Boswell were crossing happily back and forth between London and Paris to exchange ideas, England and France were at war.[11] Rarely since that time has the republic of letters flourished in such cheerful disregard of the hard realities of international politics. That this could occur in such a fashion is eloquent testimony to the fact that the age of mass involvement in politics, with entire nations mobilized and at war, had not yet arrived.

The term which is used in intellectual history to characterize eighteenth-century culture, especially in France, is the Enlightenment. This is a term which the eighteenth century itself put into circulation, and it neatly summarizes the view which contemporary writers had of themselves and what they thought set them apart from earlier ages. The eighteenth century built upon and extended the periodization of the past which Renaissance thinkers initiated, dividing European history into the Classical World, the Middle Ages (or, more graphically, the Dark Ages), the Renaissance and the Enlightenment.

Consider for a moment what this historical periodization implies. The origins of western civilization are for all intents and purposes taken to be pre-Christian Greece and Rome, which reached magnificent heights in philosophy, drama, rhetoric, and political and military organization. The level of civilization achieved by these cultures provides a kind of bench-mark for all that follows. Unhappily, what follows immediately thereafter is the gradual rise to dominance of the Catholic Church, and the institutionalization and enforcement of religious superstition and the stifling of the free play of reason. The official recognition of Christianity by the Roman Emperor Constantine (288?-337) is a dramatic symbol of the decline, and the eighteenth-century British historian Edward Gibbon was not the only one to connect the rise of Christianity with the fall of Rome. The term "The Dark Ages" is the most vivid expression of this disparaging view of the period, but the phrase "The Middle Ages" communicates the same message in muted form, implying an interim period in which history virtually stops, held fast in the grip of fixed attitudes and unbending institutions.

The Renaissance or "re-birth," of course, marks the reappearance in modern form of the norms and culture of classical antiquity. The *philosophe* d'Alembert neatly summarizes the Enlightenment's picture of European history in a passage remarking on the modern reappearance of pre-Christian forms of knowledge and culture: ". . . upon emerging from a long interval of ignorance, preceded by centuries of enlightenment, the regeneration of ideas, if we can speak this way, must have necessarily been different from their original generation."[12] A lifeline of humanist sympathy, then, is thrown over the Middle Ages and back to Greece and Rome, as writers all through the early modern period attack and deny their medieval heritage and link themselves spiritually and intellectually with the great men of antiquity. One can see that in this context the Enlightenment becomes a phrase pregnant with meaning; the eighteenth century is the efflorescence, the full flowering of authentic western culture, a period in which ignorance and superstition are overcome and the magnificent advances of the Renaissance are consolidated and fully integrated into civilized life.

One might say in a few words, then, that the Enlightenment was a powerful movement of ideas whose objective was *liberal-*

ization and whose method was *reason*. Intellectuals were driven, not to reaffirm or elaborate established modes of thought, but to confront ignorance and superstition with reason; to subject corrupt institutions and foolish practices to criticism (and often to ridicule); to enlighten, to educate mankind; to replace religious dogma with "rational faith"; and in general to free men's minds and bodies from the shackles of political and ecclesiastical authority, from "enthusiasm" or uncontrolled personal passion, and from the dead burden of the past.

Denis Diderot's monumental *Encyclopaedia,* the collective product of the efforts of more than two hundred writers from every conceivable area of enquiry, is without doubt the most comprehensive single source for the study of Enlightenment ideas. In the "Preliminary Discourse," d'Alembert writes of medieval civilization as follows:

> ...most of the great minds during those dark ages ... were preoccupied with a thousand frivolous questions about abstract and metaphysical beings instead of thoroughly investigating Nature or studying man. The solutions to these questions, whether good or bad, often required a great deal of subtlety and consequently abused the mind to a considerable extent. If you add to this great confusion and disorder the state of slavery in which almost all of Europe was submerged, the ravages of superstition born of ignorance and which reproduces ignorance in its turn, you will see that nothing was missing in the way of obstacles to prevent the return of reason and good taste; *for only the freedom to act and to think is capable of producing great works, and freedom needs only enlightenment to protect itself from excess.*[13]

Politically, the *philosophes* believed in the necessity of personal liberty for the advancement of knowledge and human welfare, and deduced from this the need for limited government. The political argument was usually cast either in natural-right or in broadly utilitarian language, but in each case it was assumed that the argument could be validated by an appeal to reason, rather than to scripture, tradition or the Divine Will. In most cases, the *philosophes* were liberals, but they were not democrats; indeed, many were advocates of enlightened despotism and some enjoyed close personal contact with such apparently enlightened but absolute rulers as Catherine of Russia and Frederick the Great of Prussia. The most renowned exception to this rule, and to most others, was Jean-Jacques Rousseau, who was a staunch democrat, and we shall have occasion to consider below his ambiguous position as a transitional figure in the shift from the Enlightenment to the Romantic era.

This cosmopolitan intellectual movement, with its belief in the practical utility of knowledge and its faith in the universality of reason and the brotherhood of man, was what many sympathetic European liberals thought was the moving force behind the upheaval in France in 1789. We have discussed above the character of the French Revolution; for many foreign contemporaries, what had appeared at first and at a distance to be the practical expression of a cosmopolitan and generous spirit of reform began to assume quite a different character as the Revolution ran its course, and indeed became virtually indistinguishable from the aggressive expression of French national interest as the armies of the Revolution marched through Europe. Instead of a fresh and bracing wind of change, German and Italian and English liberals experienced the often cynical expression of a Gallic *raison d'état* which was quite prepared, for example, to prop up reactionary regimes in buffer states along the Rhine if that suited the exigencies of France. It is, then, within the context of the traumatic effects which the French Revolution had on contemporary Europe that nationalism was born.

Germany is the obvious case in point. At the end of the eighteenth century Germany, with a residual consciousness of a common past and a common culture, had experienced a century and a half of political division and internecine squabbling. From the point of view of a concern with the origins of nationalism, there are two trends of importance in this period of German history. First, there is the establishment of the sovereignty and independence of a multitude of small German principalities at the expense of the Holy Roman Empire, an occurrence which is marked by the Treaty of Westphalia in 1648. What this meant was that, despite the continuing importance of Austria and the rise of Prussia to great-power status during this period, there were no political institutions capable of effecting the gradual unification of Germany. Second, there is the establishment in these small states of princely absolutism which precluded the emergence of constitutionalism and any elements of popular representation. The process by which this occurred was begun during the agony of the Thirty Years' War (1618-1648) and was completed in the century that followed. The result was the exclusion of the population from political activity and the creation of a deep gulf between the court and the people. As in France during the same period, this involved the obstruction of the ambition of the middle classes and intellectuals to assume what they thought was their rightful position in political affairs.

The unfortunate situation of Germany, both with respect to its fragmentation into a mass of petty jurisdictions and with respect to the princely absolutisms which covered its territory, was painfully apparent to many Germans at the time, but its consequences were brought dramatically home to them by the French Revolution and its aftermath. At first Napoleon with his armies was greeted as a saviour by many German liberals, but a reaction soon set in. Where many had expected genuine assistance from the French in domestic reorganization and reform, it soon became apparent that a weak and divided Germany suited French interests very well, and that the internal constitutional structures of the various principalities were very much of secondary concern to France.

The psychological effects of this realization were devastating for many German intellectuals and in many cases precipitated a radical re-thinking of their political attitudes and ideas. Many came increasingly to view the Enlightenment as a French rather than a cosmopolitan intellectual movement, and to interest themselves in the particular characteristics and capacities of German civilization. Out of the exploitation of German disunity and impotence by other European nations emerged the conviction that political independence and political power was an essential element of national and cultural well-being, and that it was first of all to itself and its own resources that a national community must look for assistance. In a world of sovereign states independently pursuing their own interests, self-help was not simply a virtue, but a bleak and demanding necessity. Thus liberals of that generation who began by conceiving liberal-democratic constitutional forms as universal goods, and who were prepared to unite with like-minded men wherever they might be found, ended up in many cases by restricting their concern for liberal-democracy to their own culture or even by subordinating it to the primary requirement of national independence.

Johann Gottlieb Fichte (1762-1814) provides us with a good example of the character of German intellectual life at the turn of the century. Fichte began his career as a student of Kantian philosophy attempting to correct certain of the deficiencies in Kant's doctrines. He was at the beginning an earnest francophile and supported the French revolutionaries because of his conviction that they were advancing the cause of liberty in the world. However, by 1807 his view of France, at least insofar as its effects on Germany were concerned, had considerably developed. He delivered a series of lectures in 1807—8 in Berlin which has become a classic in the literature of nationalism. The lectures, entitled *Addresses to the German Nation,* were presented while Prussia was still under the occupation of Napoleon's armies after its defeat at the Battle of Jena in 1806. An appreciation of the historical circumstances is essential to an adequate understanding of the lectures, for they seem to be informed with that acute sense of inferiority and insecurity which at times issues in pretentious claims of superiority.

In the midst of a country which is rather an aspiration than a fact, and in the aftermath of cataclysmic defeat, Fichte asserts the superiority of Germany over neighbouring European nations. Fichte argues that nations are defined by language. "It is true beyond doubt that, wherever a separate language is found, there a separate nation exists, which has the right to take independent charge of its affairs and to govern itself . . ."[14] Germany, like classical Greece before it, is blessed with an original tongue whose national purity has been only slightly sullied by foreign accretions. It is the common possession of the German language which binds Germans in different communities together and which instills in the nation a vast, prim-

itive power, a magnificent potentiality, which currently lies /
dormant but which will soon burst forth.

He contrasts the happy linguistic condition of the German
language with that of "the other Teutonic races," especially
French. These languages are artificial amalgams of Latin and
early German and as a consequence lack authenticity and are
bereft of a coherent principle of existence. "Men," he says,
"are formed by language far more than language is formed
by men."[15] This theory of linguistic purity and the constitutive
power of language has an obvious cutting edge when it comes
to the question of national identity. If languages form men
and national communities, and there are pure and impure
languages, then it is clear that the nation that is possessed of
an authentic or natural tongue will itself be authentic and
natural in a way that others will not and cannot be. Germany,
then, despite its contemporary impotence, is in fact an authentic and genuine community as was classical Greece. Such
actually powerful and coherent national communities as France
and England, however, are to be properly understood as vitiated
entities, artificial if not positively unnatural.

A further quotation from the *Addresses* exemplifies this
point and indicates how far from the cosmopolitanism of the
Enlightenment Fichte and many of his contemporaries have
moved. He is considering the way in which the Germans are
distinguished from other Teutonic peoples, and writes: "The
difference arose at the moment of the separation of the common stock and consists in this, that the German speaks a language which has been alive ever since it first issued from the
force of nature, whereas the other Teutonic races speak a language which has movement on the surface only but is dead
at the root. To this circumstance alone, to life on the one
hand and death on the other, we assign the difference."[16] And
again, with breath-taking simplicity, he writes: "Naturalness
on the German side, arbitrariness and artificiality on the foreign side, are the fundamental differences."[17]

If it is fair to identify the Enlightenment with French culture
in particular, it is reasonable as well to say that Germany was
the heartland of the Romantic movement which followed. At
the level of intellectual life, it can be seen that Romanticism,

seeded though it was in the work of certain prominent eighteenth-century figures, was both a dramatic reaction to the
most cherished presuppositions of Enlightenment thought and
at the same time a positive assertion of a novel view of the
natural and social world.

But it is impossible to restrict one's attention solely to the
world of culture. In practical affairs, the French Revolution
and the Napoleonic Wars constituted the turning point in this
period of European civilization, and were without doubt the
critical historical events in the reformulation of the European
imagination. There is an obvious national element in this
rapid process of change which may be discerned in the assumption by Germany of continental leadership in matters of
philosophy and culture. Just as the full expression of the Enlightenment spawned the Romantic era in reaction to it, so
the culmination of French hegemony at the turn of the century
galvanized other European countries (and particularly Germany) into action, and produced in neighbouring European
communities a self-conscious effort at defining themselves and
their interests in contradistinction to French civilization and
political power. Reinhold Aris paints a vivid picture of the
barren and derivative condition of political speculation in
Germany until after 1789: "The political thought of Germany
throughout the eighteenth century was based almost exclusively
on French and English sources and it took Germany a long
time to digest this alien system of ideas and adapt it to the
specific German political situation."[18] It was in the generation
that followed, and under the shattering impact of war and
foreign occupation, that the work of creation was begun.

The change was experienced on all fronts. In general terms,
it involved downgrading the things which the previous era
had thought important and bringing into bold relief the things
which it had neglected or ignored. The intellectual historian,
C. E. Vaughan, has given us his view of the character of the
transformation that took place as Enlightenment forms of
thought were supplanted by Romantic forms; it was, he says,
"a change from the spirit of criticism to that of creation;
from wit to humour and pathos; from satire and didactic
verse to the poetry of passion and impassioned reflection;

above all, a change from a narrow and cramping conception of man's reason to one far wider and more adequate to his powers."[19] It is clear, especially in the last phrase quoted, that Vaughan applauds the coming of Romanticism. A rather more neutral observer is A. O. Lovejoy, who argues that at the centre of the difference between the Enlightenment and the Romantic era is the fact that the former valued what was universal and standardized and immutable, whereas the latter valued what was individual and unique. Lovejoy suggests that a remark of Spinoza sums up a central principle of Enlightenment thought: "The purpose of Nature is to make men uniform, as children of a common mother."[20] The effort to realize nature's purpose, conceived in this way, was, in Lovejoy's opinion, "the central and dominating fact in the intellectual history of Europe from the late sixteenth to the late eighteenth century."[21] In the entire history of thought, Lovejoy asserts, there have been "few changes in standards of value more profound and more momentous than that which took place when the contrary principle began widely to prevail—when it came to be believed not only that in many, or in all, phases of human life there are diverse excellences, but that diversity itself is of the essence of excellence."[22] It is in this setting that the preoccupation with the nurturing of the peculiar genius of individual nations and races appeared, and with it the ideology of nationalism.

There is a lengthy quotation from Fichte which is worth reproducing in its entirety, for one can discern in its passionate language the mingled strains of Romanticism and nationalism:

We may say that genius in foreign lands will strew with flowers the well-trodden military roads of antiquity, and weave a becoming robe for that wisdom of life which it will easily take for philosophy. The German spirit, on the other hand, will open up new shafts and bring the light of day into their abysses, and hurl up rocky masses of thoughts, out of which ages to come will build their dwellings. The foreign genius will be a delightful sylph, which hovers in graceful flight above the flowers that have sprung of themselves from its soil, settles on them without causing them to bend, and drinks up their refreshing dew. Or we may call it a bee, which with busy art gathers the honey from the same flowers and deposits it with charming tidiness in cells of regular construction. But the German spirit is an eagle, whose mighty body thrusts itself on high and soars on strong and well-practiced wings into the empyrean, that it may rise nearer to the sun whereon it delights to gaze.[23]

This is a sustained polemic against France, against the *philosophes* and French cultural leadership, and against the leading values which provided the intellectual support of the previous age. Even in its strongly coloured language and dramatic imagery, this passage from Fichte is evocative of the Romantic era. The "foreign genius" is a delightful sylph, a busy bee, which hovers in graceful flight and is so insubstantial it will not make a flower bend; it adorns and embellishes the work of others, strewing flowers on the roads of antiquity, clothing an already existent wisdom of life; when it engages in the work of construction, it is like a bee taking up the honey from flowers and arranging it "with charming tidiness" in neat, orderly compartments. Contemporary European culture, according to the picture Fichte draws of it, is safe, unimaginative, and utterly derivative; at best it is a source of harmless adornment, an unnecessary but charming gilding of someone else's lily, and at worst it is merely trivial and irrelevant—it does not even possess the force and integrity to be positively destructive or corrupt. Like the French language, there is movement on the surface only, but no well-spring of dynamism and creativity. It is not, then, a culture of creation, but a culture of imitation, of arrangement and re-arrangement.

The German spirit in its cultural manifestations is in Fichte's view the exact antithesis of all this; it is a culture of creation with a vengeance. German civilization is a mighty natural force, cracking the very earth open and rising in reckless aspiration toward the sun. The expression of its primitive but profoundly creative power in the world is disorderly and occasionally destructive in some respects, but the result is awesome, magnificent and genuinely original. German culture exposes unplumbed depths to the light of day, hurls up "rocky masses of thoughts" which will provide materials for the civilizations to follow. What Greece did for Europe in the past, Germany will do for the Europe of the future. Germany is an eagle to France's sylph.

There is a connection between Romanticism and nationalism.

This is strong stuff. It is more than that; it is nothing short of extraordinary when we recall that these words were uttered in Berlin just after Prussia's defeat at the hands of Napoleon. It is possible that some of the French officers of Napoleon's army of occupation may have attended the lectures; one wonders what passed through the minds of any who were present when they heard these words. It is the historical context of German defeat and French victory that underlines the nationalist dimension of the Fichte quotation most clearly. Germany has been laid low, but Germany is great. Her enormous creative energy will assert itself, she will rise up and shrug off her enemies and proceed to fulfill her unique destiny in the world. The first shall be last, and the last shall be first.

The relationship of Romanticism and nationalism, and the distance of each from Enlightenment thought, may be perceived with some clarity within this single passage.

NOTES

1. Cited in L. H. Leder, ed., *The Meaning of the American Revolution* (Chicago: Quadrangle Books, 1969), p. 30.
2. *Essays on Freedom and Power* (New York: Meridian Books, 1964), pp. 146-7.
3. Ibid., p. 144.
4. "Reflections on the Revolution in France," *The Works of Edmund Burke*, vol. II, p. 284.
5. Ibid., p. 350.
6. Ibid., p. 352.
7. Ibid., p. 467.
8. See A. B. C. Cobban, *A History of Modern France* (Baltimore: Penguin Books, 1965), vol. I, p. 164.
9. Quoted in H. A. L. Fisher, *A History of Europe* (London: Edward Arnold, 1955), p. 823.
10. G. Barraclough, *The Origins of Modern Germany* (Oxford: Basil Blackwell, 1962), p. 406.
11. *Nationalism*, p. 34.
12. "Preliminary Discourse," *The Encyclopaedia: Selections* (New York: Harper Torchbook, 1967), pp. 12-13.
13. Ibid., p. 13 (my italics).
14. *Addresses to the German Nation*, ed. G. A. Kelly (New York: Harper Torchbook, 1968), p. 184.
15. Ibid., p. 48.
16. Ibid., p. 58.

17. Ibid., p. 71.
18. *History of Political Thought in Germany from 1789 to 1815* (London: Frank Cass, 1965), p. 21.
19. *The Romantic Revolt* (New York: Charles Scribner, 1907), p. 3.
20. *The Great Chain of Being* (New York: Harper Torchbook. 1963), p. 292.
21. Ibid., p. 293.
22. Ibid.
23. *Addresses to the German Nation*, p. 73.

4.   Self-Determination
        and the
        Modern Age

The language of politics feeds on analogy. Because of the extreme difficulty we experience in understanding and describing the associations and groups in which we live, the human mind resorts repeatedly to metaphor and simile. We attempt to comprehend the nature of a political phenomenon by assimilating it to something with which we are familiar, by noting that it is similar to something else. Plato thought the Greek city-state was like a work of art and that the political leader, the philosopher-king, was like an artist. Aristotle likened city-states to biological organisms and in the manner of a research scientist he set about identifying their pathologies. One can hear the organ tones of the Anglican Church sounding behind Richard Hooker's ecclesiastical polity, and the stern voice of the Roman patriarch ringing through Sir Robert Filmer's political theory. For Machiavelli and Marx, politics was war.

On the cover of the original edition of Thomas Hobbes's most famous work is a picture of that mortal god, Leviathan, sword in one hand, sceptre in the other, crown on his head, brooding over the village huddled beneath him, a Gulliver among the Lilliputians. Closer inspection of this magnificent creature shows him to be composed of nothing but the citizens of the state over which he is ruling; with a nice irony, the artist personifies the Hobbesian power which holds the citizens in awe and obedience, and suggests at the same time the source of that power—the citizens themselves.

Both the artist and Hobbes himself are making use of what is without doubt the richest and most fertile analogy which the language of politics possesses: the analogy between human groups and the human individual. It has been used on countless occasions and in countless different ways; it is fair to say that this analogy is something which we cannot do without. Consider the example of a "corporation." This is a concept which has been employed for centuries in religion, in law, in politics and social life, and in business enterprise. In legal matters, a corporation is understood to be a "legal fiction," that is to say, something which does not have an empirical reality but which is nevertheless invested with a legal status and identity to permit certain activities to be carried on and certain relationships to be established, and to allow for the defining of legal responsibilities and rights. Generally speaking, a corporation is an association of individuals which is looked upon *as if it were* a single individual in certain respects. Thus it is invested with a personality, a life of its own, a will, and very often with rights and duties under the law. Corporate officers are its representatives or agents, and they may be given the right to speak for the corporation; when they are acting in an official capacity, they are recognized to be in a position to declare the will of the association.

Now, the idea of a nation is much more informal than the idea of a corporation, but the basic analogy employed is the same. A nation, for those who are adherents of the ideology of nationalism, is like an individual, and is assumed to have in many vital respects similar drives, similar principles of action, and similar identifying characteristics. This is obviously a problematic affair, for if it is helpful to think of a nation as being similar to a human being in some respects, it is at the same time critically important to be clear about the way in which the two things differ, about where the comparison breaks down. This is a general problem with analogical reasoning, for the illumination that can be derived from an apt comparison depends as much on a recognition of the differences as it does on the similarities. Of course, if the objective is not intellectual clarity but political persuasion (as is often the case in discussions of nationalism), then confusion on this subject may be very useful and may be exploited with considerable effect.

In this chapter, then, we wish to consider in some detail the entity to which the nation is compared—the individual. If we possessed a fixed and settled conception of human nature and there was general agreement about the constitution of the individual, this would no doubt be wasted effort, for the comparative reference would be clear. But there is no such agreement; there are radically different theories of human nature, and it is upon a particular one of these that the doctrine of nationalism primarily depends. It is therefore important to realize which one it is and to appreciate what its peculiar characteristics are if one wishes to understand nationalism and nationalism's extraordinary appeal.

While it is obvious that every social and political theory must have a place within its framework for the individual, it is also the case that the position of individual persons and the attention paid to them by the theorist can be greater or less depending upon the assumptions and the overall character of the theory. In much medieval political thought the focus of attention was on God's wishes for mankind and on God's ecclesiastical and monarchical representatives on earth, while in Marxist theory politics is seen to involve the working out of a relationship of conflict and struggle between distinct economic classes. Given the focus of attention in each case, one would expect to find and one does in fact discover that the analytical significance that is attached to individual human beings recedes by comparison with the primary analytical categories.

However, as we indicated in the previous chapter, since the time of the Renaissance a preoccupation with the individual person has been one of the hallmarks of western civilization. The rise to prominence of the independent individual has been closely related to the emergence of religious dissent and resistance to traditional religious authority during and after the Protestant Reformation. And it took just a few generations for the argument that subordinate communities and individuals ought to be granted the freedom to seek God in their own way to be extended into other areas of social life. Out of this general process of change gradually appeared a tradition of political reflection which placed primary emphasis upon individual human beings distinct from their status in a hierarchical social and religious order. The broadly humanist concern of the period is reflected in myriad ways; in the rise of religious dissent and the notion of a personal search for God; in the emphasis on achievements in this world rather than on preparation for the next; in the concern with the way in which men came to know their world and the extent of their rational capacities. Much of this is summed up in Alexander Pope's famous lines in *An Essay on Man*:

> Know then thyself, presume not God to scan:
> The proper study of mankind is man.

In social and political thought, this humanist impulse took the shape of an increasing preoccupation with individual human beings as the basic unit of analysis and the entities whose welfare constituted the end of social and political life. We are today so much the product of this individualist past that it sounds odd to suggest that any other conception of society and government is possible. But of course it is; the glorification of God, for example, if it is conceived as the end of government, may involve or seem to involve the destruction of individuals, as can be seen in the long history of European religious persecution. So we must remember that the individualist assumptions which are so much a part of our age are themselves the product of a certain historical period, and not universal truths upon which all mankind is of one accord.

Nationalism appeared in the midst of this developing tradition of liberalism, and it will therefore be useful to consider briefly individualist political thought, and especially the notion of self-determination as it relates to persons as distinct from peoples. Personal self-determination has, in a sense, always been an element of political liberalism and has rested behind much of the agitation and argument for individual freedom in which liberals historically have engaged. Whether the particular practical evil has been religious intolerance, the undue interference of the state, or the tyranny of public opinion, the end of liberals who have demanded respect for personal autonomy, privacy and liberty has been the securing of the maximum possible space for individuals within which they can determine for themselves what course of action or thought they choose to pursue and what kind of life they will live.

But the stream of liberalism in the modern world has followed many distinguishable courses; for our purposes, it is useful to identify and describe two of the main trends in liberal thought. While these intellectual traditions are reflected to some degree throughout the historical period under review, each is nevertheless associated with certain writers and is particularly prominent at certain times. Let us call the first tradition the *individualism of self-protection,* and the second the *individualism of self-realization.* The first tradition was at the centre of liberalism when it first emerged in the early modern period and it has remained a theme of critical importance right down to the present day. The second was perhaps less significant at the beginning, but the idea of individual self-realization came to the fore in the course of the eighteenth century and, as the implications of this new mode of thought were gradually worked out, it altered the problems and framework of liberal theory as they had existed up to that time. The intellectual transformation which then occurred had consequences of the highest importance in social thought, and it is also of pivotal significance in understanding the historical context and character of nationalism. We have had occasion in the previous chapter to note aspects of the general alteration in European consciousness which occurred towards the end of the eighteenth century; but here our interest lies specifically in the history of liberalism during this period, and more particularly in the psychological theory of liberalism.

As the specifically religious dissent of the sixteenth and early seventeenth century began gradually to widen into claims for liberty in all walks of life, the main outlines of political liberalism began to declare themselves with increasing clarity, and a distinctive mode of discourse in political thought emerged. By all odds the dominant form of argument for advancing the individualism of self-protection during this period was that of the social-contract school or school of natural rights. The conventional style of presentation which members of this school employed involved the hypothetical assumption that men lived in a state of natural independence, outside of any political order and with none but "natural" responsibilities to their fellow creatures. Having created these hypothetical creatures, writers then considered the kind of agreement which such naturally free men could rationally assent to in the creation of a political order and the rule of law, and the introduction of a public coercive force to regulate individual behaviour. The tools of analysis which members of the school used were the non-political "state of nature," "natural rights" which people possessed by virtue of their common humanity and not by virtue of membership in a civil order, the closely related notion of "natural law" which men were able to recognize by the employment of their individual reason, and "the social contract," the agreement which free individuals made to create legitimate civil authority.

By way of example, Thomas Hobbes (1588-1679) and John Locke (1632-1704), despite the important differences in their political theories, both employed these conceptual tools and both were members of the social-contract school. The details of their arguments do not concern us here, but certain of their common assumptions about human personality and the nature of the social order are of importance in illuminating what we have called the individualism of self-protection. In elaborating their views of human nature, both Hobbes and Locke made it very clear that the persons they had in mind when they articulated their models of politics and social life were rational, mature, self-interested but not unenlightened adults. They of course excluded children and madmen from consideration, on the grounds that the first had not yet achieved maturity and the second were incapable of it. To use the language of a later era, one might say that the individuals who composed the Hobbesian or Lockean polity possessed thoroughly integrated personalities and a robust sense of identity which neither civil commotion nor personal crisis could shake. There would be small need of psychiatrists or welfare workers in the community which Hobbes and Locke had in their mind's eye. Both theorists assumed that individuals were coherent and stable units acting upon an external world, but not, as a result of their social activity, suffering assaults on their personal identity or experiencing significant alteration in their character. They may have had all kinds of problems, but they had not the slightest difficulty in knowing who they were and what they were set on earth to achieve. Generally speaking, they knew what they wanted from life, they were able to calculate how to get it, and they had a lively appreciation of the need for social order and the consequent responsibility each person had to control his conduct in such a way as not to incite the violence or antagonism of his fellows. This, then, was the picture that Hobbes and Locke and many other liberals during the period drew of their fellow man; if for the most part he was devoid of grandeur and magnificence, if heroic struggle and cataclysmic victory or defeat were alike unknown to him, he was nevertheless possessed of the moderate virtues of commonsense and prudence. He sought the quiet life in politics that he might secure autonomy and success elsewhere.

As far as the political order was concerned, liberals in this tradition established to their own satisfaction that personal consent, rather than custom, inheritance or divine will was the basis of legitimate government. But it was *consent* and not self-government that was the legitimizing principle; while they deemed it essential that a government, whether it be monarchical or republican, be grounded in the free and rational acceptance of the people, they did not in most cases require democratic constitutional structures. As we have seen in the previous chapter, many Enlightenment intellectuals continued in the eighteenth century the tradition of individualism which was developed in the sixteenth and seventeenth centuries. Just as they assumed that human nature was stable and not impossibly complex, so they took it as a matter of course that the ends of government were durable, finite and intelligible to all rational men. Thus, for writers in this tradition, what was important was not so much who made the decisions, but whether they were the right decisions. They were more concerned with good government than with self-government.

Hobbes and Locke, together with many other contemporary liberals, sought to limit and define the powers of the state; they sought to restrict public activity primarily to those areas which were necessary to preserve peace and to allow private men to get on with private measures. Their theories of liberty were consonant with their attitudes to men and the political order. Liberty was very much a "freedom *from*" affair; it was freedom from the interference of one's fellows, freedom from unnecessary restrictions of the government—in general liberty meant the securing of a domain of privacy in which man could advance his own interests unfettered and unencumbered by the demands and actions of others.

Now, as we have suggested, out of this tradition of social and psychological reflection there emerged a significantly different pattern of thought which we have identified as the individualism of self-realization. On the surface it appeared to be carrying on the line of thinking charted by seventeenth and early eighteenth-century liberals, but in reality its problems and its positive doctrines constituted a significant departure. Indeed, the notion of self-realization not only became a novel element of decisive importance in liberalism, but it also emerged as an important factor in a host of modern movements and social theories such as philosophical idealism, socialism, existentialism and, as we shall indicate, nationalism.

Jean-Jacques Rousseau (1712-1778) is in this respect a critical transitional figure. He put his fertile imagination to work as a political and educational theorist, a novelist and a musician, and in virtually every endeavour struck a deep response in European consciousness. In speaking passionately and eloquently for himself, it turned out he spoke the unspoken thoughts of many of his contemporaries, and in consequence he placed himself at the head of a new wave of culture in western civilization.

So far as the story of liberalism is concerned, Rousseau employs all the instruments of analysis of earlier liberal theory (the state of nature, natural rights, the social contract and so forth), but he takes up these tools only to transform them and apply them to new tasks. At every point his thought is straining to pass beyond the confines which these categories of analysis impose. In his psychological speculation Rousseau introduced a novel element into the discussion, and one with a turbulent and disruptive future. Earlier writers such as Locke and Hobbes were of course primarily concerned with the security and happiness of individuals, but their theoretical enterprise was directed to establishing satisfactory external arrangements to provide people with the necessary conditions for the pursuit of the good life. They took the character and composition of human beings very much as a given and, once they had settled to their own satisfaction the unchanging psychological principles and drives of men, they proceeded to construct their political theories on that solid foundation.

Rousseau, however, was not content to treat human psychology as a fixed and established thing so far as politics was concerned, and as a consequence to restrict his attention to the best external pattern of relationships that could be conceived. Rousseau was fascinated with his own psychological condition; he was very often disturbed by what he discovered about himself during his exercises in introspection, and he assumed that what he learned about his own character and identity was generally applicable to his fellow human beings as well. An unchanging human nature ceased to be the fixed centre around which all political theory turned and became one variable among many others, and one moreover which was more often than not badly in need of drastic alteration if the desired political system was to prevail; political theory and social psychology became very closely linked in Rousseau's speculation. He introduced personal identity, "the self," into political discussion as one of the problems with which politics had to deal, and this ghostly and elusive entity has hovered in the political atmosphere ever since.

Rousseau had two important insights in this connection. First, he argued that it was not possible to discern fixed and unchanging principles of human behaviour which would permit political speculation on a firm basis of empirical reality; human personality was seen to be extraordinarily complex and subject to drastic change in different times and circumstances. Secondly, Rousseau believed that there was a deeply influential reciprocal relationship between man and society. The conceptual model with which many early liberals worked was one in which individuals were treated very much as the unchanging atoms out of which were built society and the state; the assumption was made that individuals in the state of nature would behave according to the same principles as individuals in civil society. Rousseau's view was radically different, and in a way that attaches him much more to us than to his predecessors. He was profoundly aware of the socializing effect of human society and insisted that men are as much the creatures of the social experience they have known as they are expressions of some immutable human nature.

Rousseau's celebrated *Discourse on the Origins of Inequality* is a dramatic presentation of his view of human nature and the constitutive role that civilization or culture in the broadest sense plays in the creation of men. In it Rousseau goes back to the state of nature of Hobbes and Locke in quest of natural man, but when he reaches what he believes to be the genuine origins of mankind he finds not man but a human-shaped beast. It is from this unpromising beginning, from *l'homme sauvage,* that he proceeds to construct his account of the emergence of *l'homme civilisé,* and the major constitutive element that Rousseau sees at work is the social order itself which over the centuries has produced the creature we know as man today. Unlike almost all of his contemporaries, however, Rousseau viewed the historical process as one of degeneration rather than progress, and took the view that the advance of civilization involved the corruption of human nature. Thus when Rousseau turned from psychological speculation to political thought, he was faced with a situation in which both culture and human nature were corrupt and in conflict with the potentialities of mankind, but he was also confronted with the fact that men were not deficient or evil by nature (that is, necessarily and universally), but rather by virtue of their social experience. The degeneration had occurred over time and could presumably be reversed.

With the introduction of the "problematic self" into political discussion in this way, liberal theory could no longer restrict itself to its traditional problems. The task of politics could no longer be seen as one of maintaining order and restricting interference in the free activity of private individuals, whether that interference came from other individuals or the state itself. What confronted politics and liberal theory now was much more daunting; it was the stark necessity of first of all creating the conditions which would make a free society possible, and this involved the reciprocal transformation of both man and society. The state could not be regarded simply as a regulating force, but as an initiating and educating power whose legitimate activities (even within the terms of liberalism) could involve immediate interference for the sake of long-term social and individual welfare. If man were alienated from himself or from society, then the first job was one of integration, one of bringing men back together again. The end of the state was not so much liberty but *liberation* for individuals—liberation from the slavish attitudes and practices which life in a corrupt society had produced in them, and liberation (in conjunction with their fellows) from a social and political order which warped and stifled human potential.

So far as individual freedom is concerned, there are in Rousseau's mind two negative conditions which have to be fulfilled. First, a person must not be subject to the will of another; and second, he must not be enslaved by his passions. The first condition is one which was important in the earlier liberal tradition, although it should be noted that many thinkers in that tradition were in fact prepared to subject themselves and their fellows to the will of a sovereign power in certain specified areas in order to be free of external controls in other areas. The second was not in any way an important consideration in the individualism of self-protection; if men were driven by greed or fear, this was an immutable principle upon which political structures would have to be built, not an unfortunate failing which could be corrected by the social order. However, a theory of human freedom within the tradition of individual self-realization involved both the right pattern of relations among persons and the right pattern of relations within the soul of each man. In the *Social Contract* (I, viii) Rousseau describes moral liberty as that which alone makes man "truly master of himself; for the mere impulse of appetite is slavery, while obedience to a law which we prescribe to ourselves is liberty." Here it is in a nutshell. If an individual is to be morally free, he must not be the slave of his own appetites and passions, and he must not be subject to the will of another. But there is a positive element of central importance as well, and it is to be found in the idea of a man giving the law to himself. What this involves is the free and independent determination of the conditions of a person's own existence and, even more important than that, the autonomous realization of individual potential. What invests the fulfillment of human potential with moral worth is the fact that the thing is done in freedom; it is *self*-fulfillment, defined and executed by the individual of his own free will.

It is this view of morality and freedom which the German philosopher, Immanuel Kant (1724–1804), discerned in Rousseau's thought and developed into an elaborate and influential moral philosophy. As Ernst Cassirer points out in his essay on the two eighteenth-century thinkers, it is at first glance astonishing that the methodical, disciplined German philosopher could have admired and respected the erratic genius of Rousseau, but it seems clear that it was because Kant was able to see beneath the outrageous personality and brilliant, paradoxical literary style of Rousseau to the underlying moral earnestness that animated Rousseau's writings and tortured him throughout his life.[1] Kant's teaching and writings were a major factor in establishing the credentials of the doctrine of self-realization and were a formative intellectual influence upon the first generation of German nationalists.

The speculative relevance of Rousseau's doctrine of self-realization in the formation of the ideology of nationalism was more immediate than Kant's, however, for his main work in social thought was in the field of politics rather than ethics, and he explicitly advanced a theory of collective self-determination which is known as the General Will.[2] We shall examine this theory in a bit more detail in a moment; here it is sufficient to say that Rousseau's concern with morality and personal liberation led him in his political thinking—if we may put it this way—from liberalism to democracy, and encouraged him to move away from a position of unvarnished individualism to one of "collectivism," albeit collectivism in the service of individual freedom and well-being. Rousseau's General Will, then, is the first systematic presentation of a theory of *collective* self-determination to parallel the theory of *individual* self-determination which was then developing. What is more, it has remained an idea of critical significance in social thought since it was first articulated in the eighteenth century by Rousseau. It provided a dramatic account of how one might conceive of political collectivities possessing a will of their own which was quite distinct from the individual wills of any of the members, and an identity and direction which was composed of the interests and purposes of individual citizens but which nevertheless transcended them.

So far as nationalist doctrine is directly concerned Rousseau made two major contributions which, if they had been fully integrated with one another, would have come very close to constituting a coherent nationalist ideology. But he kept them separate, and he did so because his primary values and goals were not nationalist, but liberal and democratic. The first major contribution is to be found in his preoccupation with patriotism and national identity, a preoccupation which appears here and there in much of his work, but especially in his work on Poland. The second, as we have suggested, lies in his theory of the General Will.

Both issue out of his lifelong concern with human freedom and self-government. One can obtain a sort of negative outline of his political theory by noting the things (and they were many) to which Rousseau was hostile. He made his reputation in the eighteenth century by his brilliantly articulated opposition to all the settled opinions of intellectual France. His views, ultimately, could not be contained within the general ambit of *philosophe* thinking, despite the fact that the *philosophes* themselves were cheerfully engaged in dismantling the structure of conventional opinion, and the widening gulf between them and Rousseau led finally to a decisive break. Rousseau's first publication assaulted head-on some of the most cherished attitudes of his time. He attacked the sophisticated and elegant civilization of upper-class Europe (and especially France), arguing that it stifled nature and repressed or distorted the beneficial natural instincts of mankind. He removed the source of evil from its traditional place in Christian theology, in the soul of fallen man, and relocated it in society, in the relations that exist among basically good men. This was a theme which was picked up and developed in different ways by many nineteenth-century anarchists and socialists. He was opposed to large social structures of any kind because they destroyed

simplicity and openness and carried with them a train of evils
—social distance, inequality, pride and envy, indirection and
complexity. The increasingly centralized nation-states in Western
Europe attracted his contempt: "I see all the states of Europe
hastening to their doom."[3] He preferred the tiny community of
Corsica to Great Britain or France; he detested Paris and ideal-
ized the city-states of Switzerland; he ridiculed the English
parliamentary political system which was then the wonder of
Europe, and applauded instead the sterner simplicity of Calvinist Geneva—or, even better, ancient Sparta or Rome. "The
people of England regards itself as free; but it is grossly mistaken; it is free only during the election of members of parliament. As soon as they are elected, slavery overtakes it, and it
is nothing. The use it makes of the short moments of liberty
it enjoys shows indeed that it deserves to lose them."[4]

This hostility to large institutions and representative political
systems is an important indicator of Rousseau's central concern. He was prepared not only to condemn the existence, but
actually to advocate the dismemberment of the large, centralized
state which was becoming more and more the typical form of
political organization in Europe. And he was prepared to do
this because he could see no other way in which his supreme
political values, freedom and self-government, could be realized
in the world. Had his major preoccupation been nationalistic
in character, his posture vis-à-vis nation-states would have been
quite different; in fact, however, he was an advocate of a system
of small city-states linked together in a loose federal structure.
Switzerland, not France was his empirical model.[5]

Rousseau's preoccupation with patriotism and national identity must be understood within this general context. When he
began to work out his liberal political theory, he discovered not
only that the political systems he saw in operation were woe-
fully inadequate, but that the men, the citizens who operated
them, were radically deficient as well. He came to realize that
the institutions of a legitimate system of government in which
freedom and the General Will could flourish would involve the
radical transformation of the whole society, the renovation of
both the state and the citizens.

It was his realization that the health of the community was

the pivot on which everything else turned that fostered his belief in the importance of what one might call the non-rational links of human association. He reckoned that if people were integrated or bound together by a distinctive language, common historical experience, customs and practices which were peculiar to that specific group of people, and so forth, then the likelihood of their possessing the energy, public spiritedness and sense of common good necessary for a state to function according to the principles of genuine self-government would be vastly increased.

In most of his writings this dimension of his thought appears in a general concern about the customs and traditions of a country, and whether they can be expected to advance or retard the introduction of legitimate political rule. For example, in the *Social Contract* (II, xii), Rousseau speaks of morality, custom, and above all public opinion rather than normal legislation as forming the real constitution of the state. Public opinion or belief, he says, is "a power unknown to political thinkers, on which nonetheless success in everything else depends."

In the case of Poland, however, he was asked to recommend a system of law for a state which was in his opinion far too large, too enfeebled and in many ways too corrupt to approximate in any way his ideal society. And yet the Poles were struggling to be free, to throw off the yoke of Russia and Austria. Rousseau was amazed to see a country which, by all the indications of political science as he understood them, should be locked in reaction and half-dead from oppression, but which was nevertheless buoyantly seeking to liberate itself and to set up a system of legitimate government. "As one reads the history of the government of Poland," Rousseau writes, "it is hard to understand how a state so oddly constituted can have survived so long. I see a body of great size: many of its members are already dead, and the remainder have no unity, so that their motions, well-nigh independent of each other, far from serving any common end, cancel one another out. . . . But Poland, depopulated, devastated, and oppressed, wide-open to its aggressors, in the depths of misfortune and of anarchy, still shows all the fire of youth. It makes bold, as if it had just sprung to life, to demand government and laws! Poland is in irons but is busy discussing means of remaining free. . . ."[6]

In his recommendations for Poland, Rousseau shows himself to be the very model of caution and circumspection. He recognizes that as an outsider his ideas must be tested very carefully by those who know the country in detail and at first hand, and in view of the extraordinary nature of the Polish experience, in which institutional corruption and foreign oppression are combined with the most sublime thirst for liberty, he argues that Poland would be foolish to engage in wholesale change because of the danger that the good might be destroyed with the bad.

His proposals, therefore, are perhaps more directly nationalist in character than those which one will find anywhere else in his writings. On the assumption that it is the peculiar genius of Polish culture which has sustained the vigorous libertarian spirit, he argues that the national identity of Poles should be protected and nurtured. ". . . *national* institutions. That is what gives form to the genius, the character, the tastes and the customs of a people; what causes it to be itself rather than some other people; what arouses in it that ardent love of fatherland that is founded upon habits of mind impossible to uproot. . . ."[7]

In the quotation below we begin to hear the authentic tones of nationalism, in the assertion of national exclusiveness and particularly in the emphasis on the nation realizing itself, cultivating its autonomous, distinctive character, and fulfilling its latent potential: "In national character, in form of government, in customs, in language, Poland is quite unlike its immediate neighbours, and the rest of Europe as well. Now: I should like Poland's military organization, its tactics, its discipline, to be unlike theirs too. I should like Poland to be, in all these respects, itself, not some other country; for only by being itself will it become all that it is capable of being, and draw forth from its bosom all the resources it is capable of possessing."[8]

Here is a perfect example of the paradoxical element in the doctrine of self-realization, whether it be personal or national— a self which by struggle will become more fully itself: "only by being itself will it become all that it is capable of being." One can see why, given the importance of the idea of self-realization in nationalist ideology, it is possible to have nationalism without a "nation."

But Poland was a special case for Rousseau, idiosyncratic in itself, and calling as well for the application of a general political theory to an actual empirical case. This accounts for the increased emphasis on nationalist factors in his analysis, although it should be remembered that the ground of his nationalism and his political caution was liberal, and his object was a system of freedom and self-government for the Poles.

The second element in Rousseau's political thought which we need to consider briefly is his theory of the General Will. We have seen that Rousseau assimilated personal liberty to the idea of self-rule, the object of which was the unfettered realization of a person's potential. Individual freedom was not just a matter of having one's natural rights to property and security protected; it was also a condition in which the individual himself formulated the rules by which he lived. He who determines for himself the conditions of his life and the principles of his operation may be considered free. But a fearsome task faced Rousseau when it came to translating this view of moral liberty into a theory of political freedom; he had somehow to relate this idea of individual self-realization to a person who was a member of a political order. How could a community of individuals, each of whom was autonomously ruling himself, regulate its collective affairs? It was in response to this dilemma that Rousseau developed his concept of the General Will.

He sets out his theory of the General Will in his famous political treatise, *The Social Contract,* which opens with the ringing declaration: "Man is born free; and everywhere he is in chains." His objective throughout is to maximize the liberty of the individual. He asserts that he wants to reconcile *freedom* and *government,* and the only way he can see of doing this is through a system of *self*-government. Thus Rousseau's concern with individual self-determination, when it is transposed to political affairs, led him to popular sovereignty in the form of the General Will. Political liberty could no longer be understood in terms of self-protection as freedom *from* government intervention except in limited, specified areas, in the way that it had been conceived by Hobbes, Locke and others; political liberty had necessarily for Rousseau to include freedom to engage in politics and government. The full flowering of liberalism for Rousseau meant the appearance of radical democracy. If people were not directly involved in government, how could it possibly be said that they were self-governing? As far as Rousseau himself was concerned, the critical element in his theory of the General Will was the direct participation of the individual in law-making so that the collective decisions of a community could also be regarded as in some sense personal decisions, so that political rule became a form of self-rule. However, for the nationalist the critical thing in Rousseau's famous concept was the coherent articulation of a theory of corporate will, and one moreover which was not necessarily dependent on the prior existence of a state or formal political jurisdiction. Rousseau's theory could thus be understood to invest a group of people with a corporate identity and with the active attribute of will, regardless of whether that group presently enjoyed political or legal definition. The General Will, then, proved to be a fruit ripe for nationalist plucking, although in Rousseau's mind it was not at all a nationalist idea.

This conception of political freedom as self-government has become increasingly popular in recent years in the West and has manifested itself in a wide-ranging critique of the conventional forms of representation and in the growing demand for personal participation in decision-making. The difficulties involved in introducing significant elements of participation and control into the gigantic social structures—the business corporations, the governments, the trade unions and universities—which compose our social world are being recognized, although some people believe that the answers will be found in the mastering of technology. On this issue, Rousseau was unequivocal; he believed that it was utterly impossible to graft participation onto the modern state and onto large social institutions. This was why, as we have seen, he quite seriously suggested the break-up of the increasingly centralized nation-states of western Europe and the creation of a mass of small republics in their place. His pessimisim was grounded in the accurate perception that no such development in the European social and political system could be expected to occur. Had he valued liberty and participation less, his tolerance of the existing state system would have been greater; this was not a problem for the early nationalists, however, because they were preoccupied with the strength of the national community and situated personal liberty in the context of collective values, especially national independence.

With the coming into prominence of the doctrine of self-realization, mankind ascended to new but often vertiginous heights of liberty. No longer could morality and freedom be understood to involve voluntary subordination to universal norms of behaviour. For centuries the European mind had assumed the existence of a law of nature which provided a transcendent moral framework within which the empirical facts and the aspirations of western culture could be situated and understood. But in the notion of self-realization as we have described it above, there is little place for natural law. Man is free in a radical sense which would have shocked the ancients; he stands naked and alone in the universe carving out his own destiny for himself—not simply adhering to fixed moral principles, but constructing for himself the moral principles which he will then freely obey, determining not only what he shall do, but what he shall *be* in the future.

In Rousseau's political thought, for example, the General Will supplants natural law as a criterion of behaviour. The important thing to notice about the shift is that a transcendent criterion which is understood to be external to man is replaced by an immanent criterion which is the creation of man, and a creation moreover which is always doing and never done. It is not surprising that during this period a revolution in religious opinion occurs; the traditional belief that God created mankind is turned precisely on its head by many thinkers, to be replaced by the contention that men created God, or belief in God, out of their own need to believe.

This, then, is a freedom which knows no limits beyond those which the free being imposes on itself. It was in particular this version of liberal theory, this conception of human nature and liberty, that fed and supported the doctrine of nationalism.

NOTES

1. *Rousseau, Kant and Goethe* (New York: Harper Torchbooks, 1965). See also Cassirer's *The Question of Jean-Jacques Rousseau* (Bloomington: Indiana University Press, 1963).
2. Elie Kedourie (*Nationalism*, ch. 2), however, sees Kant as the central figure in this respect.
3. *The Government of Poland*, ed. W. Kendall (New York: Library of Liberal Arts, 1972), p. 2. See also p. 25.
4. *Social Contract*, III, xv.
5. In Canada today, George Woodcock typifies this Rousseauist impulse with his dislike of nationalism and the centralized state, and his concern to foster the emergence of small, "human-sized" communities in free association with one another. See the stimulating discussion between Woodcock and some other Canadian writers in *Canadian Forum*, April 1972.
6. *Poland*, p. 2.
7. Ibid., p. 11.
8. Ibid., p. 80.

5. Nationalism and Liberal Democracy

We are now in a position to address ourselves to an issue that for some time has hovered on the fringe of our discussion and which is influential in defining attitudes to the national question —the relationship between liberal democracy and nationalism. Many writers, both liberal democrats and nationalists, insist that the two are inextricably connected, and in the nineteenth century this was for the most part simply assumed without argument; both a nationalist like Mazzini and a liberal like John Stuart Mill agreed that liberty for individuals and liberty for nations were simply different aspects of a single comprehensive liberal theory. Other writers, especially in the twentieth century when the destructive capabilities of nationalism have become more apparent, have argued the reverse, that nationalism and reaction go hand in hand. Is one of these views correct?

Two links between nationalism and liberal democracy are evident from what we have said so far. First of all, it can be admitted straight away that the two patterns of thought are creatures of the same historical period; it is reasonable to assume, therefore, that ultimately they share a common ground in some of the most basic assumptions and features of the modern age. But to suggest that the creation of the conditions suitable for the emergence of each involved the waning of religious belief, for example, or the gradual emergence of what has been called mass society, or advances in the technology of communication—this does not establish a connection of great significance between the two, especially when one realizes that communism and fascism are products of the modern age and share much the same ground in these respects as well.

Secondly, it can also be pointed out, as we have done above, that nationalism turns on an analogy with the human individual, explicit or implied, and that the argument and justification for the self-determination of nations parallels at many points the theory of individual self-determination. Clearly, this is a finding of some importance and with it we come, or seem to come, a step closer to establishing a substantial link between the two ideas. Certainly it is the attachment by analogy of nationalism to a popular and compelling conception of human personality that gives it much of its appeal and much of its political force.

But our specific concern here is to consider whether, as is often asserted, there is a necessary connection between liberal democracy and nationalism *as political doctrines*; and here, I think, the answer must be that there is none. Nationalism is a doctrine which is concerned with the position of the nation vis-à-vis other nations and other groups, and within this doctrine there is no necessary assumption which need be made concerning the set of relationships which obtain among the individuals who compose the nation or between the individuals and the community as a whole. These relationships, however, are precisely the ones which are central to any liberal-democratic theory. To the extent that there is any "natural" direction at all to the doctrine of nationalism, it is one which involves the depreciation of the individual and his concerns relative to the nation as a whole.

Indeed, what can be said with confidence is that *as a doctrine* nationalism must set national liberation above personal liberation as a value. It may be argued (and often is) that the freeing of the nation or the possession by a nation of sovereign powers for itself may be more conducive to individual welfare and liberty than any other arrangement. But for a nationalist this must be a statement which, however important, is logically subordinate to the primary issue, which is the welfare and liberty of the nation; whereas for a liberal democrat this statement, if he believes it, will provide him with a reason for combining with nationalists because of his assumption that the advancement of nationalist goals will further what is for him the primary issue, the struggle of the individual for freedom.

It is from this latter direction that nineteenth-century England's most renowned liberal, John Stuart Mill, arrived at his support of the nation-state. "Free institutions," he wrote in Chapter 16 of *Considerations on Representative Government*, "are next to impossible in a country made up of different nationalities." And again: "it is in general a necessary condition of free institutions that the boundaries of governments should coincide in the main with those of nationalities." In view of Mill's belief that liberty produces diversity and diversity in its turn preserves liberty, it might seem surprising that he was an advocate of the nation-state; but it is pre-eminently diversity of opinion and belief that he has in mind, and not cultural pluralism.[1] However, another great Victorian liberal took precisely the contrary view of the nationality question. Lord Acton, in his famous essay "Nationality," began from a position of general agreement with Mill about the interrelationship of liberty and social diversity, but he arrived at quite different conclusions: "The co-existence of several nations under the same State is a test, as well as the best security of its freedom. It is also one of the chief instruments of civilization . . . , and indicates a state of greater advancement than the national unity which is the ideal of modern liberalism." [2]

One can see that it is possible for a liberal today to draw on quite distinct strands in his heritage so far as the national question is concerned. A vigorous case for the nation-state and for national liberation can be built up on the basis of John Stuart Mill's argument. And a trenchant critique and alternative position can be constructed out of the statements of Lord Acton.[3] Both sides of the question of whether nationalism is a liberal or illiberal force have been argued persuasively and with sophistication, but I should like to suggest that both rest upon a mistake, namely, the assimilation of nationalism to a scale of values associated with a different political doctrine. Mill sees nationalism as a liberal and progressive force, Acton views it as reactionary; but in reality it is neither. The categories of progressive and reactionary, left and right, liberal and illiberal, cannot be applied in general terms to the doctrine of nationalism, and the allocation of praise or blame along those lines rests on a misconception of what the doctrine is about.

Nationalism, like any other political ideology, has a specific "moral thrust," but it is incorrect to assume that its view of the world and its prescriptive direction are in principle either consistent with or contrary to the goals of liberalism. Given the assumption of nationalist ideology that national self-government is legitimate government, and the empirical fact that nations are not all as yet nation-states, the major "ethical" and operating principle may be readily discerned: the right of nations to self determination. This is a distinctively *nationalist* principle and, as we shall suggest below, it is not possible to deduce from it any specific, logical relationship between nationalism and liberalism, or indeed between nationalism and socialism, fascism or any of the other prominent modern ideologies.

This is not to deny the obvious fact that specific nationalist movements in specific countries may have a character and may possess social and political goals which make it possible to describe the movement as reactionary, or liberal, or left-wing. Clearly, it is possible and perfectly reasonable to do this, but it can only be done by looking at the specific political movement "down on the ground," so to speak, by examining the actual empirical form in which nationalism manifests itself and the other social forces with which it is allied. This involves studying the individual country with its indigenous institutions and problems, its peculiar history and traditions, its particular situation in the world at large, and so forth, because what one is in fact commonly faced with is a complex mixture of political forces and values, only one element of which is nationalist. In such a case the conclusion as to the liberal or reactionary character of the thing under inspection will relate to the concrete and untidy political movement or regime, bastard son of a hundred different motives and purposes, rather than to a pure empirical example of the phenomenon "nationalism."

A mistake on this point may have serious consequences, and an example may be found in Canadian experience in the case of Pierre Trudeau. Trudeau, a liberal schooled in the anti-nationalism of Acton, and shaped by his generation's experience of fascist tyranny in Europe and reactionary Duplessisism in Quebec, takes the unequivocal position that nationalism is an intrinsically right-wing, regressive force in the world and therefore to be resisted by liberals and socialists everywhere.

So far as Quebec is concerned, few would quarrel with the view that the brand of nationalism articulated by Duplessis and his long-standing Union Nationale government was illiberal in character. To those opposed to the dominant social and political tendencies of Duplessis' Quebec, it must have seemed at the time as if the forces of progress were struggling against a reactionary nationalism which gripped French-Canadian society and engendered a stultifying traditionalism and social immobility. But however adequate this analysis may have been in explaining French Canada in the 1950s, it is quite seriously wide of the mark in the 60s and 70s; for during the Quiet Revolution right-wing nationalism was supplanted by liberal nationalism as the dominant force in society, and it may be that further changes are in store—for example, in the developing linkage between socialism and nationalism in Quebec. Someone who believes it is possible to establish that nationalism is *by nature* a reactionary force will, by virtue of that very fact, be committed to fundamental misunderstanding and serious distortion when faced with the complex patterns of nationalism which are currently gripping French-Canadian society.

The issue can be clarified by a fuller consideration of the theories of John Stuart Mill and Lord Acton. Mill views the right of national self-determination in oversimplified and distorted terms as a simple deduction from a comprehensive liberal political theory: "Where the sentiment of nationality exists in any force, there is a *prima facie* case for uniting all the members of the nationality under the same government, and a government to themselves apart. This is merely saying that the question of government ought to be decided by the governed. One hardly knows what any division of the human race should be free to do if not to determine with which of the various collective bodies of human beings they choose to associate themselves."[4]

This position seems unimpeachable if one assumes a world in which states are being constructed *de novo*; but in a world in which the territory is already divided up and the people are all presently members of one political order or another, it is surely sophistical and often in practice disruptive even of legitimate political societies. On Mill's argument, not even the sentiment of nationality is necessary for this theory of self-determination to come into play; any group of people, however defined, who evince a settled desire to associate themselves with a specific political jurisdiction or to construct a new one ought to be permitted to do so.

However, whether the group is defined in national or other terms, Mill's argument takes little account of reality. There is almost no place on the face of the globe that is not part of some state's sovereign territory and this is a fact of the greatest significance in considering Mill's argument. Whatever the validity of the nationalist's claim that nature created and defines nationality, it is indisputable that *citizenship* is determined by convention and is in fact the creature of law. It is quite intelligible to say that a given citizen body, defined by a particular set of political and legal circumstances, possesses the right to determine for itself what kind of system it will live under. It is quite another thing to assert that a segment of that citizen body may unilaterally determine what political arrangements it will accept and what sovereign authority it will recognize.

The citizen body constitutes that population in a country which possesses political rights and which is entitled to participate in the political process. In a democratic country there is at least a *prima facie* case for saying that a decision which would affect the constitution as profoundly as the decision of a minority to secede must be arrived at democratically, which is to say, by consultation with the whole citizen body. Indeed, if there is an extraordinary procedure to be followed at all in such a case, it might very well consist, not in the acceptance of the unilateral decision of the minority, but in the suspension of the normal representative procedures so that the entire community could express itself on this crucial issue. (There are obviously in practice limiting factors of great significance, particularly when the minority is defined by nationality, which is why we speak of a *prima facie* case. The limiting factors and the most satisfactory context within which to place a secessionist movement will be dealt with subsequently.)

A tacit assumption in Mill's argument is that the nationality which possesses the right of self-determination is concentrated in some distinct region or territory. It would clearly make little sense to speak of black Americans enjoying a right of self-determination which included the option of state secession when in fact there is no black territory or homeland within the United States which could be ceded. The right of emigration and the possibility of setting up a new community elsewhere (as in the case of Liberia) can be readily admitted, but this is quite a different matter. Self-determination in this case is obviously subjected to pronounced structural limitations.

Mill, then, was restricting his attention to a cultural or other minority group of a rather specific sort: either one which was not already under some formal political organization or else one which occupied a distinct territory within a given state or empire. However, we have noted that the former case is abstract and unreal, for in the modern world there are no longer any territories or populations of any magnitude which are not politically organized. As for the latter case, that of a minority which occupies a distinct territory within a state, its position in the larger community does involve the issue of consent, but consent of a particular kind, and not simply and exclusively consent. When Mill suggests that accepting the right of national self-determination is "merely saying that the question of government ought to be decided by the governed," he is only giving us part of the story and is neglecting features of critical importance which complicate an issue of this kind in real life. There are differences of the first importance between working out the relationship of a cultural minority to the whole community on the one hand and deciding upon such issues as the selection of government leaders, the level of taxation in the country or the direction of foreign policy on the other. It is evident that for a liberal democrat consent is the primary source of legitimacy for all the issues mentioned in the previous sentence, including the minorities question, but one of the things at which liberal-democratic thinkers have not excelled is the distinguishing of various forms and degrees of consent and the diverse conditions in which it must be understood to operate.

Edmund Burke's famous attack on the abstract individualism of the social-contract school is germane here. "Society is indeed a contract," Burke wrote. "Subordinate contracts for objects of mere occasional interest may be dissolved at pleasure —but the state ought not to be considered as nothing better than a partnership agreement in a trade of pepper and coffee, calico or tobacco, or some other such low concern, to be taken up for a little temporary interest, and to be dissolved by the fancy of the parties."[5] Breaking up a country is not only different from trading in pepper or calico; it is different from such subordinate political activities as electing a Liberal or Conservative government, or deciding on whether or not there shall be military conscription; and this fact must surely be reflected in the procedures and institutional arrangements that are employed to determine consent in each case.

The French writer Ernest Renan wrote in the nineteenth century that a nation is "une plébiscite de tous les jours," a daily plebiscite.[6] In one sense this is true not only of nations, but of all forms of human association; they all depend for their existence on at least a minimal degree of willingness on the part of their members to tolerate the continuance of the association. Were this minimal acquiescence absent, the thing would fly apart. But one may conclude that Renan meant rather more than this. He speaks of "the clearly expressed desire to continue life in common," and here he appears to be suggesting the active affirmation and re-affirmation of a will to perpetuate a common existence. But if this is meant to indicate a form of consent which could be transformed overnight into opposition, into the withholding of consent, then it is more misleading than illuminating. Human institutions are not in reality subjected to daily plebiscites, especially not such durable natural-artificial entities as the nation and the state, and the danger here is that an inappropriate metaphor may lead to a misapprehension of the phenomenon itself.

Burke used the image of a partnership to suggest the missing dimension in the consent theory of social contract, but a partnership of an entire political community and of succeeding generations. The state, he wrote, "is a partnership in all science; a partnership in all art; a partnership in every virtue, and in all perfection. As the ends of such a partnership cannot be obtained in many generations, it becomes a partnership not only between those who are living, but between those who are living, those who are dead, and those who are to be born."[7] If it can be said that the seventeenth and eighteenth-century natural-right theorists stretched the idea of contract until at last it snapped, it may also be suggested that Burke's argument ultimately does violence to the concept of partnership, investing, as it seems to do, life and will in the dead and unborn. Nevertheless, it does effectively serve to remind us that political communities, while dependent and properly so on the will of their members, are also grounded in something more substantial and less evanescent than individual will, or even the momentary collective expression of will of a part of the community. The image of a language is perhaps more appropriate than that of partnership, for communities, like languages, are the product of the convergence of will and circumstance. No individual is responsible for the creation of a language; it emerges in the course of time through usage, accident and haphazard arrangements, and eventually becomes emblematic of a substantial group of people. If Fichte is referring to individual human beings when he speaks of "men," then there is an important element of truth in his statement that men are formed by language far more than language is formed by men. But equally true, of course, and only superficially paradoxical, is the assertion that language is the creation of men, that is to say, of human collectivities. John Stuart Mill himself recognized in the first chapter of *Representative Government* that neither the understanding of society as a machine and the product of human will, nor the understanding of society as an organism and the product of nature was adequate on its own, and that the truth lay somewhere between, but he failed to apply this insight to his brief discussion of nationalism.

We have argued that the theory exemplified by Mill which connects liberal democracy and national self-determination is not satisfactory. Let us now consider the contrary position, the most prominent exponent of which is Lord Acton, namely, that a nation-state is an illiberal form of political organization and that there is an important relationship between cultural pluralism and political liberty. It is an attractive and plausible theory when stated in general terms, but unfortunately there is far too much empirical evidence against it for it to withstand scrutiny.

Acton was one of the most erudite and thoroughly cosmopolitan of Victorians. The product of a union of noble English and European families, Acton spent his youth at family residences in Italy, France, Germany and England and spoke each of the four national languages fluently. He was a Whig and a Catholic, and spent a good deal of time and effort attempting to reconcile the often apparently conflicting requirements of these two faiths. It is primarily his political liberalism that we are interested in here, although it can be noted in passing that he took the view that one of the secular benefits of Christianity was the way in which it broke down the national barriers between man and man and encouraged the transcending of the exclusive ties of race, blood and ethnicity. Such political theorists as Machiavelli and Rousseau agreed with Acton about the effects of Christianity, but were for that reason opposed to it on the grounds that universal religious attachments would compromise the community affections upon which a healthy polity was based.

Acton's liberalism was typical in most respects of his age; where he differed from the bulk of his contemporaries was in his hostility to nationalism, whose course in European history he observed acutely and whose potential dangers he discerned and described in detail. But his ethnocentrism was as strong as Mill's, and he shared with Mill and many other Victorians what appear today to be some rather uncritical assumptions about "progress" and the steady "advance" of Western civilization. It was in this progressive context that he situated his admiration for the multinational state. "The combination of different nations in one State," Acton wrote, "is as necessary a condition of civilized life as the combination of men in society. Inferior races are raised by living in political union with races intellectually superior. Exhausted and decaying nations are revived by the contact of a younger vitality. Nations in which the elements of organization and the capacity for government have been lost . . . are restored and educated anew under the discipline of a stronger and less corrupted race. . . . Where political and national boundaries coincide, society ceases to advance, and nations relapse into a condition corresponding to that of men who renounce intercourse with their fellow men."[8]

One can see in this quotation that Acton the anti-nationalist accepts and employs the analogy between the nation and the individual, although he puts it to work to combat the doctrine of nationalism. It may also be suggested that his use of this analogy leads him into distortion. Specifically, his argument carries two mistaken implications: first, that creative, "progressive" relationships do not obtain among members of the same nationality, but only between members of different national groups; and secondly, that creative "inter-national" association can take place, as he says, only "in the cauldron of the State," and not between nationalities in different states. If both of these points were true, it would of course provide impressive support for his argument, but they are not. Indeed, if by way of example we confine ourselves to the arts, it may be convincingly argued that some fields of creative endeavour, such as music and dance, are decidedly international in character, and transcend not simply the regional cultures within a single state, but draw their vitality from beyond the level of the state itself. On the other hand such creative activities as literature and drama are deeply dependent upon a particular national culture and indigenous artistic tradition for their development. It is indisputable that the nation-state has become the organizing focus for cultural life in the modern world as the city-state and the imperial centre were the focal points for the cultural life of earlier civilizations.[9]

Besides, if we can indeed accept the view that social diversity is important in maintaining a free society and a high level of cultural life, there are nevertheless a variety of forms other than the strictly cultural which might be expected to carry with them similar benefits. In Canada, for example, in addition to the fact of cultural pluralism, there are important class differences, and distinctive regional and religious identities which would appear to be as significant in awakening and sustaining the creative imagination as linguistic and ethnic differentiation have been. This is particularly plausible in the case of a country such as Canada in which the various cultural identities have traditionally been heavily insulated from one another. In any case, the twentieth century has become much more skeptical than the nineteenth about the existence of a universally applicable standard of progress in terms of which the level of civilization in all societies can be measured, and the existence of such a standard is a vital presupposition which gives point and purpose to the case Acton is seeking to establish.

Acton's objective as a liberal was to set limits to the authority of the state so that diversity and individual liberty could flourish. He saw any "holist" ideology or single-minded purpose (nationalism included) as a threat to free society: "Whenever a single definite object is made the supreme end of the State, be it the advantage of a class, the safety or power of the country, the greatest happiness of the greatest number, or the support of any speculative idea, the state becomes for the time inevitably absolute."[10] A liberal, then, seeks to protect and nurture "the establishment of great independent authorities not derived from the State,"[11] and Acton sees the existence of more than one nation within a given political jurisdiction as the most effective of all barriers to the centralization, corruption and absolutism toward which all states tend.

Unfortunately, the record of history appears to contain at least as much evidence to undermine as to sustain the thesis that the multinational state is a buttress and the main buttress of liberty. The homogeneous community of the Netherlands is certainly not less liberal and humane than its binational neighbour, Belgium. Switzerland has indeed provided an impressive example of the combination of liberalism and cultural pluralism, but the multinational state of South Africa has not. The origins of the Spanish parliamentary system are as ancient as those of Great Britain, and the Catalan and Basque nationalities are as distinctive as the Scottish and the Welsh, but the constitutional history of the two countries has been very different indeed.

Acton at one point contrasts the French and the English political systems and suggests that the latter demonstrates that theory of "national liberty which belongs to the theory of freedom,"[12] in other words, an instance of the understanding of the proper relationship between nation and state. But this is puzzling. Whether one regards contemporary Great Britain as a single nation or as a culturally plural society of English, Welsh, Irish and Scottish, it seems evident that the happy constitutional development of Great Britain has not been in any significant degree the direct result of cultural pluralism. Britain has for centuries experienced the contrasting traditions of local and regional autonomy on the one hand, and vigorous centralization on the other, and it may very well be that the development and maintenance of liberty has been related to the tensions and interplay of these traditions. Neither localism nor centralization has been solely or especially related to the existence of more than one nationality in the state; indeed, both of these traditions have been as much social and constitutional in character as anything else, and can be seen in such institutions as the common law and the local administration of justice, the system of parliamentary representation, and the monarchy.

In contradiction of the Actonian thesis, the major stain for generations on Britain's liberal constitution has been the direct result of conflict between nationalities. Not only has Britain been unable to resolve the Irish question, it has never been able successfully to establish a just and liberal constitutional system in Ireland. Part of the problem was dealt with by secession, but the bitter religio-national struggle continues between Ulstermen and Irish Catholics in the North. Here the diversity which, according to the Actonian thesis, should be the buttress and mainstay of freedom has destroyed it.

I would suggest that in modern history ethnic and cultural diversity has more commonly produced conflict and racial tension than tolerance and harmony. Switzerland is the exception to the rule, Ireland a violently hued instance of its application. Even if it can be substantiated, as it may, that the probabilities in this matter are themselves created in part by the universal and disruptive appeal of nationalist ideology, the sombre facts remain and must be faced by anyone who wishes to understand contemporary nationalism or to cope with its effects in the world. National diversity within a political community has frequently issued in the reverse of a liberal regime, and in a system of oppression which corrupts the majority while it stifles the minority.

It is important to emphasize that there is nothing inevitable about this process. In many cases liberty has flourished where national diversity has been absent or uninfluential. In some cases the two seem to have gone hand in hand, and in still others the presence of a number of nationalities within a single state has led to civil war and fragmentation, or has on all the evidence retarded the development of mutual tolerance and respect for human rights. In our effort to understand nationalism we are thrown back once again upon the need to examine specific cases and to avoid excessive generalization. On one point we can wholeheartedly agree with Lord Acton, however: the coexistence of several nations under the same state is without doubt a test, and a very stringent test, of its freedom. But we cannot go on to assume with him that it is its best security.

Nationalism, then, is a distinct political doctrine, with a mode of analysis, a scale of values and a political impetus which are peculiar to it. It is fallacious to view nationalism as a subordinate clause in the grand statement of liberalism; and it is equally fallacious to view it as a force which is implacably hostile to all forms of personal liberty and individual welfare. It is neither of these things. Kenneth Minogue, in the closing paragraph of his book on the subject, catches very well the inevitable ethical ambiguity of the thing: "There is room for both the Sleeping Beauty and the Frankenstein's monster view of nationalism. It brings millions of people out of traditional corners into the global commerce of the modern world, and it induces a psychological climate conducive to bitter, irrational struggles over contested bits of territory. The good it does could all be done in other ways; but equally, it has contributed little more than a new vocabulary to the history of political evil."[13]

NOTES

1. There are tensions between Mill's general statements and what he has to say about certain specific cases, for example, in his writings on Ireland and Ireland's place in Great Britain. I do not believe that Mill ever satisfactorily resolved the matter.
2. *Essays on Freedom and Power*, p. 160.
3. Both strains of thought have been amply represented in Canada throughout her history. One of the most significant figures in nineteenth century Canadian history, and indeed in British imperial history of the period, was an English statesman whose Whig credentials were fully as good as Mill's and whose opinions were broadly similar. Lord Durham, "Radical Jack" as his contemporaries nicknamed him, applied the logic of the main stream of English liberalism to Canada with unstinting energy and confidence. In his celebrated *Report* Durham advocates a policy of assimilation of the French-Canadian community, and he does so, to employ Acton's words, in pursuit of that "national unity which is the ideal of modern liberalism." Canadians today have in their midst a prominent and self-conscious Actonian liberal in the shape of Pierre Trudeau.
4. *Considerations on Representative Government,* Ch. 16.
5. "Reflections on the Revolution in France," *The Works of Edmund Burke*, vol. II, p. 368.
6. See excerpt from Renan's writings in Hans Kohn, ed., *Nationalism* (New York: Anvil Original, 1965).
7. Burke, *Works*, vol. II, p. 368.
8. *Essays on Freedom and Power*, pp. 160-1.
9. A brief and fascinating essay which explores the relationship between culture and social diversity is T. S. Eliot's *Notes Towards the Definition of Culture* (London: Faber and Faber, 1962). Two intriguing studies of Canadian literature and culture are: Northrop Frye, *The Bush Garden* (Toronto: House of Anansi, 1971), and Ronald Sutherland, *Second Image* (Toronto: New Press, 1971).
10. Acton, *Essays*, p. 159.
11. Ibid., p. 151.
12. Ibid., p. 158.
13. *Nationalism* (Baltimore: Penguin Books, 1970), pp. 154-5.

6. Self-Determination in International Relations and International Law

If the eighteenth century saw the first appearance of nationalism, the nineteenth experienced the full expression of nationalist doctrine in Europe. A movement of ideas whose influence was initially confined primarily to intellectuals and literati gradually penetrated into the ordinary population and attitudes of Europe. What occurred during these fateful years was that nationalism proved itself to be a doctrine of widespread and magnetic appeal, a set of ideas which was capable of reaching and motivating large groups of people, and politicians and intellectuals were not slow to recognize the necessity of some kind of accommodation. Many European statesmen and political leaders assimilated nationalism to beliefs which they held on other grounds or wove it intricately into the ongoing affairs of state. A few saw it as a keg of political dynamite and reckoned that, even if they could not make it go away, they should at least approach it with circumspection and respect.

Increasingly in the nineteenth century the national question was on the negotiating table in European political affairs, jostling uncomfortably with other issues, but claiming attention with ever-increasing stridency. The Italian *Risorgimento* and the overall thrust towards Italian unification under the leadership of Mazzini, Garibaldi and Cavour which took place in the middle years of the century were vigorously and obviously nationalist in character, and there were clear elements of a developing German nationalism in the gradual unification of Germany under Prussian leadership. Also, the constitutional and political upheavals of 1848 which spread like grassfire through the capitals of Europe, while predominantly liberal in their direction, very often manifested distinct nationalist overtones as well.

Two other occurrences of significance which took place during this period might be noted, although they were not directly nationalist in character. First of all, a major wave of what we have come to know as decolonization occurred with the liquidation of the Spanish and Portuguese empires in South America in the 1820s and the appearance of a number of independent republics in that part of the American hemisphere. Secondly, in the early 1860s the United States fought a bloody civil war to resolve by force of arms the question of whether member states had the right to secede. The right of independence which the Thirteen Colonies claimed in the eighteenth century was denied to some of the states of the Republic in the nineteenth. This evidently was not a nationalist struggle, although it was a conflict between two quite different ways of life; but it was a dramatic indication in the first modern federal country of the difficulties which lie in the way of communities which wish to counterpose centralization and regional autonomy, unity in certain matters and diversity in others. It was, as well, a warning to other countries which might contemplate the genuine division of the state's sovereign power that a true federal system might require for its successful operation a political maturity beyond the reach of man, or an absence of political problems which no one in this world had a right to expect. The Canadian Fathers of Confederation pondered the lessons of the American Civil War deeply a few years later, with what degree of success we shall shortly consider.

Given the great and increasing worldly success of nationalism during this period, advocates of liberal and socialist societies had somehow to cope with the doctrine, either by reconciling it with their own political theories or by confronting it directly and showing it to be a mistaken and reactionary force in the world. As we have seen, liberals for the most part took the first course of action, with the result that the tensions that existed between their theories and nationalism remained covered over and obscure for generations. Socialist thought has traditionally been trans-national in perspective although, as we have already noted, socialists share with nationalist thinkers an antipathy to the atomistic individualism of early liberal thought. In any case, the structural economic analysis and internationalism of socialist thought makes an ultimate reconciliation with nationalism very difficult indeed.

Nevertheless, the fact that socialists have found it necessary to effect a doctrinal marriage of convenience between socialism and nationalism provides further evidence of the strength of the latter in European politics in the nineteenth century and world politics in the twentieth. Complete autonomy for all nationalities was enunciated in the 1896 program of the London Congress of the Second International, and formal recognition of the right of peoples to national self-determination was included in the 1903 platform of the Russian Social Democratic Workers' Party. Both Lenin and Stalin wrote a good deal on the question of nationalities, and this of course was a complex and delicate issue with which the Bolsheviks had to contend in their accession to power in Russia. Indeed, the 1936 federal constitution of the Soviet Union included the theoretical right of secession for the constituent republics, although its practical unreality prompted one contemporary observer to remark irreverently: "The apostles of secession have unfettered freedom as nationalists, but they will be shot as revolutionaries."[1] The USSR has in fact been one of the most vigorous supporters of the right of national self-determination in international affairs, although its application of the right is highly selective, as can be seen in the way it has dealt with nationalist movements within its own sphere of influence.

In conjunction with the rising importance of the phenomenon of nationalism in the nineteenth century there gradually developed a more coherent and settled vocabulary to describe the doctrine and the various political movements which marched forth under its banner. Acton, in his essay of 1864, did not speak of "nationalism" but of the "principle of nationality," which amounted to much the same thing. And although the idea of national self-determination was in fact coeval with the doctrine of nationalism itself, it is primarily the twentieth century which has seen the full blossoming of the phrase "the principle (or the right) of national self-determination," and which has witnessed this terminology enter not only the ordinary language of politics and international affairs, but has also seen it emerge as a controversial and increasingly important legal concept in the field of international law.

There have been two periods in this century when the doctrine of self-determination has assumed special importance in world affairs.[2] The first is the period during and just after the First World War, when the focus of attention was on the European land empires of Russia, Turkey, Austria-Hungary and Germany which were defeated or which collapsed in the course of the war. The communities to which the concept of self-determination was applied were the culturally and linguistically defined nationalities of central Europe as well as certain territories in the Middle East. Nationalist agitation was rife in central Europe during the war, and with the encouragement or acquiescence of the United States and her allies this sentiment was an important factor in the creation or reconstitution of such states as Poland, Czechoslovakia, Rumania and Yugoslavia—not all of them, be it noted, nation-states.

The second period, which followed the Second World War, saw the focus of attention shift to the overseas empires of the European powers. The world has experienced a process of decolonization lasting three decades and one which is only now drawing to a close. What a complex and mammoth undertaking this has been is suggested by the fact that well over fifty non-selfgoverning territories have acceded to independence since the United Nations was formed, most of them during the 1960s. Perhaps the major cases yet to be resolved in this general decolonizing process are the Portuguese territories and the white-settler minority regimes of southern Africa, each of which possesses certain significant distinguishing characteristics.

The pivotal figure of the World War I period, and probably the most significant single public figure in the story of self-determination in this century, is Woodrow Wilson, president of the United States from 1913 to 1920. Wilson, at one point in his career a prominent political scientist, had elaborated for himself a comprehensive view of the world. This view suffered some adjustment and manhandling when he went into politics, of course, but it remained throughout his public life an influence of the greatest importance. One dimension of Wilson's political theory manifested itself very clearly in his foreign policy, particularly in his enunciation of United States' objectives in the First World War and the consequent policy which flowed from it. His influence was profound in the 1919 Versailles Peace Conference which followed the termination of hostilities and in the construction of the League of Nations which grew out of these meetings.

One might describe his political beliefs as an amalgam of stern Calvinist morality and a tempered Jeffersonian democratic theory. The son of a Presbyterian minister, Wilson never lost the deep religious faith with which he had been imbued as a child, and he assumed without question that the ethical framework of the state in its international relations was identical with that of the individual in his personal relationships with his fellow man. This belief emerges clearly in his repeated declarations that the United States had nothing to gain from the war and was pursuing in the conflict only those interests which were shared universally by mankind. "We have nothing material of any kind to ask for ourselves. . . . Our interest is only in peace and its future guarantees."[3] "May I not add that I hope and believe that I am in effect speaking for liberals and friends of humanity in every nation and of every program of liberty? I would fain believe that I am speaking for the silent mass of mankind everywhere who have as yet had no place or opportunity to speak their real hearts out. . . ."[4] The United States, then, in its relations with other powers, was not pursuing a narrow concept of national interest, but was striving to realize the general good of all (within which America's good might be found), and thus to further God's will in the world.

This lofty idealism, which was at least intelligible while the United States remained neutral in the European conflict, became perplexing and a constant source of confusion and misunderstanding for both the Allies and the Central Powers once she had entered the war. The idea of the United States, "the prize amateur nation of the world,"[5] as President Wilson described it, fighting a war to further no national interest, but spending its blood and treasure altruistically to serve the interests of mankind, was a difficult notion for old Europe to grasp. Here is President Wilson requesting Congress to declare war on Germany: "The world must be made safe for democracy. . . . We have no selfish ends to serve. We desire no conquest, no dominion. We seek no indemnities for ourselves, no material compensation for the sacrifices we shall freely make. We are but one of the champions of the rights of mankind . . . we fight without rancor and without selfish object, seeking nothing for ourselves but what we shall wish to share with all free people."[6] One would almost think from this part of his address that American lives had not been lost and American shipping not interfered with by German submarines. The presence of such a man at the peace negotiations, actually representing one of the parties to the conflict, was bound to have an unsettling effect, not least because, whether Wilson was conscious of it or not, there *were* American interests at issue and American purposes being served.

With this strong moral conviction was combined an abiding faith in the virtue and intelligence of the people, of ordinary people everywhere, and a consequent insistence on democratic government as the only proper form of political organization. Wilson throughout his life was hostile to institutions of social privilege and inequality and to all governments which were not firmly grounded in the consent of the people. His conception of appropriate forms of representative political institutions was thoroughly Anglo-Saxon, and he had little appreciation and less respect for the different political arrangements which other cultures and other societies appeared to require. Legitimate government was liberal-democratic government on the American style, perhaps on the British, and conceivably on the French style, and he was confident enough of this fact to be willing to employ United States' influence and military power in a foreign country to ensure that legitimate political rule as he understood it could prevail.

Wilson's "democratic altruism" informs United States' policy in Central and South America during his tenure of office, and is particularly apparent in his disastrous intervention in Mexican affairs during the Mexican Revolution—a series of threats, truculent assertions, and armed "incidents" which led ultimately to General Pershing's futile punitive expedition of 1916–17. The motivations for this solicitous American concern were the purest. The president himself stated that the objective of American policy was "to help Mexico save herself and serve her people."⁷ In the same statement Wilson declared that "the people and Government of the United States cannot stand indifferently by and do nothing to serve their neighbor. They want nothing for themselves in Mexico. Least of all do they desire to settle her affairs for her, or claim any right to do so. But neither do they wish to see utter ruin come upon her, and they deem it their duty as friends and neighbors to lend any aid they properly can to any instrumentality which promises to be effective in bringing about a settlement which will embody the real objects of the revolution—constitutional government and the rights of the people." Within a single paragraph Wilson shuttles back and forth between a declaration of non-interference (the United States has no right to settle Mexico's affairs for her) and a warning that, if the Mexicans don't do it for themselves, the United States may in fact *have* to settle Mexico's affairs for her and secure for her the "real objects" of her revolution. A recent commentator uncovers with ruthless clarity this paradoxical and recurring element of American foreign policy. Of Woodrow Wilson's Mexican dilemma he writes: "Wilson had arrived at that fatal recurring moment in our country's diplomatic benefactions, the moment when it makes sense to start shooting people philanthropically, for their own good. He was as ready to do Mexicans this service as we have proved, year after discouraging year, with Vietnamese. . . ."⁸ Indeed, there is a discouragingly contemporary ring in Wilson's outburst to his Secretary of State about then President Gomez of Venezuela, whom Wilson cordially detested: "This scoundrel ought to be put out. Can you think of any way in which we can do it that would not upset the peace of Latin America more than letting him alone will?"⁹

Wilson was able to move smoothly from a theoretical position of non-interference and respect for the right of self-determination to a practical position of the most direct intervention in the domestic affairs of other states with the help of his democratic nationalist beliefs. America never moved against the *people* inhabiting foreign countries, but always against their *governments*. The objective was always to undermine or destroy governments which were despotic and illegitimate according to Wilsonian political theory or, as in the case of Mexico, to make a troubled country "safe for democracy." Thus interference was not really interference (except for the corrupt regimes), but actually assistance generously offered to the people or the nation as a whole in their effort at self-determination.

When Wilson proceeded unilaterally to make America's war aims clear, it was this complex of democracy, nationalism and morality that he was seeking to advance, all of them in his view interconnected. The European conflict then in progress (and in fact most previous modern wars as well) had been brought on in his opinion by the petty bickering of irresponsible political leaders ruling despotically over European states and empires. The people had not been consulted and the people had not advised; in a very real sense for Wilson, the people of the various countries were not belligerents, despite the fact that it was their blood that was being spilled on the fields of battle ("we have no quarrel with the German people,"[10] "we are . . . the sincere friends of the German people,"[11] "We have borne with their present Government through all these bitter months because of that friendship . . ."[12]). Wilson was confident that peace and international concord were clearly in the interests of all mankind, conflict and military conquest in the interest of irresponsible rulers alone; certainly he as the chief executive of the democratic United States of America had nothing to gain from an aggressive and expansionary foreign policy, and he presumed that other democratic countries would be similarly and pacifically disposed. So a rational as well as a humane and morally defensible foreign policy was one which sought to ensure that the postwar world would be one composed of states whose authority was based on the freely given consent of their citizens and in which democratic political institutions prevailed. One can see how Wilson's conception of political reality committed him to a foreign policy which had to include specific concern with the internal organization of foreign states.

Given these views, it is no surprise that, when Wilson came to enunciate his Fourteen Points in an address to Congress in January 1918 (after unsuccessfully attempting to secure a joint statement of Allied war aims), he included as a central plank in his platform the principle of self-determination of peoples. "An evident principle runs through the whole program I have outlined," Wilson declared at the end of his address. "It is the principle of justice to all peoples and nationalities, and their right to live on equal terms of liberty and safety with one another, whether they be strong or weak. Unless this principle be made its foundation no part of the structure of international justice can stand."[13] In his own mind, Wilson conceived this principle primarily, but not solely, in liberal-democratic terms, although he certainly agreed with John Stuart Mill that *national* self-determination is simply one element in liberal theory. The simple clarity of the principle as it appeared in Washington, however, vanished in a fog of confusion and obscurity in Europe, where the problems associated with nationalism and liberalism were intricate and vast, and where a great many different meanings were placed upon the specific principle, many of them incompatible or at odds with the Wilsonian concept of free government.

An examination of the Fourteen Points, and the four supplementary points which President Wilson later announced in a speech in July 1918, reveals a wide variety of specific cases which are, in the president's view, covered by the principle of self-determination of peoples. There is the restoration of full sovereign independence to Belgium (Point VII), and the erection of an independent Polish state which would include "the territories inhabited by indisputably Polish populations" (XIII). There is the adjustment of the Franco-German border (VIII) to rectify the wrong done to France by Prussia in 1871 in the matter of Alsace-Lorraine (the wishes of the population are not specifically mentioned here), and "the readjustment of the frontiers of Italy . . . along clearly recognizable lines of nationality" (IX). The peoples of the Austro-Hungarian and of the Ottoman empires are accorded "the freest opportunity of autonomous development" (X), "the absolutely unmolested opportunity of autonomous development" (XII). Russia, then in the throes of revolution, was to receive from the comity of nations of the postwar world "the unhampered and unembarrassed opportunity for the independent determination of her own political development and national policy and . . . a sincere welcome into the society of free nations under institutions of her own choosing" (VI).

In Point V Wilson proclaimed with exquisite ambiguity the "free open-minded, and absolutely impartial adjustment of all colonial claims, based upon a strict observance of the principle that in determining all such questions of sovereignty the interests of the populations concerned must have equal weight with the equitable claims of the government whose title is to be determined." Although the meaning of this statement is not by any means self-evident, it would seem that the emphasis here has shifted from the people to the government, in part perhaps because of the paternalism which Wilson evinced for backward peoples such as the American negroes and which, as we shall see, is clearly present in the colonial clauses of the League of Nations Covenant. He was doing little more than following nineteenth-century liberals like Mill and Acton in this. The government to which Wilson is referring in Point V seems quite clearly to be the relevant European imperial power, and it is significant in view of his emphasis on popular sovereignty that Wilson speaks of the *interests* rather than the *wishes* of the colonial population. All of this is consistent with the fact, which soon became apparent, that when Wilson (and the Allies generally) spoke of self-determination they had in mind European nationalities and not colonial populations, at least not the colonial populations of the victorious Allies. The colonies of the defeated powers were another matter, although it was more a matter of a transfer of authority than the granting of independence. In a speech in September 1919 Wilson admitted: "It was not within the privilege of the conference of peace to act upon the right of self-determination of any peoples except those which had been included in the territories of the defeated empires."[14] As Alfred Cobban points out, this was a damaging admission, for it amounted to an acknowledgment that the victors were insisting on the application of a moral principle to the vanquished which they refused to apply to themselves.[15]

Throughout the Fourteen Points and the four supplementary points there is an obvious antipathy to absolute and irresponsible government, and a veiled hostility to empire; on the other side, there is a transparent commitment to democratic political constitutions and to the nation as the appropriate unit of political organization. Wilson does not speak of states, but of "peoples," collectivities which possess some non-political principle of unity. Behind all he says about the new postwar world of peace and justice which he desires for Europe is the necessary assumption of the empirical existence of European nations or peoples which can be identified and separated from one another, which possess a will of their own whether or not they presently enjoy the benefits of independent government, and which are thirsting for freedom and self-government. He was soon to discover that this complicated assumption was problematical in the extreme and that, even if it were accurate, the practical difficulties obstructing its concrete realization were enormous. And I think it can fairly be said that we have learned enough since Wilson's day to be skeptical about the healing and pacific powers of an international policy of liberal nationalism.

Even within the framework of the Wilsonian declaration itself there are statements which it is not easy to reconcile with the principle of self-determination. We have noted already the apparent exclusion of the colonial empires of the victors from the application of the principle. Also the reservation of free and secure access to the sea for Poland was an undertaking assumed without regard to the desires of the people who inhabited what was to be the Polish corridor. But if Wilson was unable strictly to adhere to his main principle even in the general enunciation of his foreign policy, still less was he able to live up to its requirements in real life. His policies and example gave hope to struggling nationalities everywhere, many of which beleaguered him with requests for assistance; but more often than not (as, for example, in the case of subject nationalities of the Allied Powers) he was constrained to ignore or refuse them. He was not much assisted by his colleagues at the peace conference, although the Allies were in general prepared to subscribe to self-determination in the abstract and the British were ready to see it applied in Europe but certainly not in the British Empire. As Cobban wryly states: "the British and American delegations were anxious to confine self-determination to Europe, while the French and Italian delegations would have preferred to confine it to Utopia."[16]

Nevertheless, the issue of self-determination arose repeatedly at the peace conference in Versailles, where President Wilson took a leading role, and most of the conceptual difficulties associated with nationalism descended with a vengeance on the discussions.[17] First of all, there was the problem of establishing what was to be understood as a nation for the purpose of the conference, and, once this was done, of drawing up fair and accurate national frontiers. National minorities in the newly formed nation-states were inevitable, and the question necessarily arose as to whether such minorities or very small cultural communities could justifiably claim the right of self-determination. A second difficulty was to be found in the tension that existed between the conception of nationality in terms of distinct language and culture on the one hand and in terms of popular will on the other. We have seen how important this second view of the nation was to President Wilson and one might have expected the very extensive use of the plebiscite as a means of determining the wishes of the population concerned. But in fact the Allies were not especially keen on this procedure. A number of plebiscites were held, but in many cases self-appointed national leaders were permitted to speak for their communities and a heavy reliance was placed as well on the identification by experts of ethnic and linguistic frontiers.[18] Unreliable enough in the best of circumstances, a single plebiscite can readily be seen to be a thoroughly unsatisfactory device for securing the settled opinion of populations shattered by years of bloody conflict. Finally, a deep uncertainty was felt among many about the way in which self-determination and the sovereign independence which that apparently implied might be reconciled with the restraints on freedom of action that an international system of order and peace seemed to require.

The Versailles Peace Conference, then, and the eminent world statesmen who attended it, legitimized as never before the principle of national self-determination as a practical rule of action; during this short period it moved to the centre of attention of international politics, a position from which it has not been long absent ever since. A British historian, writing just prior to the Second World War, summed up the termination of the First in this way: "The war against the German Empire ended in a radical and revolutionary peace drawn up by democratic politicians. It recognized the liberation of nations, canonized new republics, provided for the protection of minorities. The general trend of Europe towards nationalism and democracy, which had made itself felt ever since 1848 with steadily increasing emphasis, seems to culminate naturally in Mr. Wilson's peace."[19]

An essential component of Mr. Wilson's peace was the creation of a world organization of states to foster and sustain collective security and peace. The idea of such a world organization had been in existence for many years, but the opening decades of the twentieth century and the bitter experience of the First World War turned an apparently utopian ideal into a deeply felt need and, in the opinion of many people, into a practical possibility.[20] Such unofficial organizations as the United States League to Enforce Peace and the British Fabian Society and League of Nations Society were simply the more prominent among the many bodies and individuals who were advancing the idea and drawing up plans for a possible world organization during the war years. Both the British and French governments established committees to consider the question and make proposals, and the South African Defence Minister, General Smuts, issued an influential pamphlet on the subject in the weeks just prior to the opening of the peace conference.

However, Woodrow Wilson, who lent his enormous prestige to the concept of a world organization, was undoubtedly the prime mover behind efforts to create the League. It was Wilson who produced the first official version of the Covenant (a word chosen by the American president and rich with associations in Protestant and liberal history), and it was Wilson more than anyone else who pushed the thing relentlessly through to its conclusion. He successfully insisted that the creation of the League be considered a fundamental task of the peace conference and that the League's "constitution," the Covenant, be an integral part of the Peace Treaty.[21]

The final version of the Covenant makes no specific mention of the principle of self-determination, and when it deals with at least one of the categories of cases which might seem amenable to the application of this principle (that of colonial territories), it appears to resort to a demonstrably different operating assumption, namely, that of trusteeship. Article 22 of the League Covenant deals with the overseas possessions of the defeated powers and opens with the following statement: "To those colonies and territories which as a consequence of the late war have ceased to be under the sovereignty of the States which formerly governed them and which are inhabited by peoples not yet able to stand by themselves under the strenuous conditions of the modern world, there should be applied the principle that the well-being and development of such peoples form a sacred trust of civilization and that securities for the performance of this trust should be embodied in this Covenant."[22] The article goes on to state that this sacred trust could best be acquitted by vesting the tutelage of such peoples in the advanced nations who can best undertake this responsibility, and indicates that specific arrangements need to be made for the various colonial communities who are at different stages of development.

The concept of trusteeship which animates the League's approach to colonies is the virtual reverse of the principle of self-determination. A trustee is responsible, not directly to the beneficiary, but to a third party in the exercise of the trust, and the relationship is one which is designed to provide for the furthering of the *interests* of the beneficiary, but not necessarily the following of his *will*. It is a paternalist relationship in which the welfare of the beneficiary is not determined by the beneficiary himself, but by agents acting on his behalf. In the case of the colonies and territories of Germany and

Turkey, then, certain advanced nations, which had been victorious in the war, assumed the role of trustee and were required to provide annual reports of their trusteeship to the Council of the League.

These "mandated territories," as they were known, were divided into three groups, based on their respective stages of development. "A" mandates applied to the Arab countries which formerly belonged to the Turkish Empire and which were fairly close to being ready for self-government; "B" mandates applied to former German colonies in central Africa which were deemed to be less developed; and "C" mandates applied to ex-German territories in South-West Africa and the Pacific Islands which, for a variety of reasons, were considered to be still further removed from the possibility of self-government and which were to be administered as integral parts of the mandatory power's territory.

The employment of this paternalist approach to colonial questions is best understood, not as a rejection of the principle of self-determination, but a tacit recognition on the part of the drafters of the Covenant that self-determination was in their opinion applicable to certain societies but not applicable to others, that the principle was relevant to "civilized" cultures, but had no bearing on backward or primitive communities. It is a general position identical to that of John Stuart Mill and his justification of empire; Mill argues that his theory of liberty does not apply to "those backward societies in which the race itself may be considered in its nonage. . . . Despotism is a legitimate mode of government in dealing with barbarians, provided the end be their improvement, and the means justified by actually effecting that end."[23] Thus national independence and liberal democracy had their place, and a very important place it was, in the discussions at the Versailles Conference and in the treaties that issued from it, but the undeveloped countries were not included, except from the perspective of an indefinite future when the necessary conditions of civilization had been established.

The arrangements which were concluded at the peace conference called for the formal ratification of the treaty by the respective home governments, including approval of the Covenant of the League of Nations itself. The bitter irony was that the country which had been the major architect of the peace and of the design for postwar reconstruction refused to approve the treaty which had been negotiated and provisionally accepted at Versailles. The United States Senate, controlled by a narrow Republican majority hostile to Wilson, declined to approve the treaty and as a consequence the United States remained outside the League and incapable of influencing the functioning of the new world organization. Many students of the period have seen this as an event of critical significance in defining the shape of the interwar years and crippling the effectiveness of the League. At any rate, during the period which followed, the League of Nations concerned itself from time to time with a number of issues relating to nationalism and self-determination, including the protection of minorities within nation-states and the operation of the mandate system.

One particularly relevant occurrence was the Aaland Islands dispute of 1920-21 which arose between Finland and Sweden. Finland exercised *de facto* control and claimed sovereignty over the Islands whose indigenous population was overwhelmingly Swedish. Sweden contended that the Aalanders wanted to join Sweden, and therefore requested a plebiscite to determine national title to the territory; Finland, on the basis of its claim to sovereignty, rejected this proposal, arguing that it was a matter of domestic jurisdiction. A Committee of Jurists appointed by the League and later a Commission of Rapporteurs both found in favour of Finland, and argued (to quote the latter): "To concede to minorities either of language or of religion, or to any fractions of a population, the right of withdrawing from the community to which they belong, because it is their wish or their good pleasure, would be to destroy order and stability within States, and to inaugurate anarchy in international life. . . ."[24]

The second wave of self-determination begins with the signing of the United Nations Charter at San Francisco in June 1945. It is clear that attitudes both in the West and in the colonial territories were maturing in the interwar years, and it is likely that the statements of allied objectives during the Second World War raised the hopes of many peoples in many parts of the world regarding the significance and general applicability of the principles of self-determination and national independence.[25]

If one were asked to characterize in a few words the situation during this second period, it would only be a slight exaggeration to say that in post-World War II international affairs, self-determination and decolonization have come to mean virtually the same thing. This is to some extent reflected in the United Nations Charter. As in the case of the League Covenant, a system for the internationally supervised administration of non-self-governing territories was provided for in the Charter, but it is significant that the paternalistic element is drastically reduced. One of the basic objectives of the trusteeship system, as enunciated in Articles 73 and 76, is to promote in the trust territories "progressive development towards self-government or independence," and explicit provision is made for taking into account "the freely expressed wishes of the peoples concerned"; these phrases in particular have been the focal point for much controversy between the anti-colonial and colonial forces in the General Assembly.[26]

In addition, the Charter explicitly enunciates the principle of self-determination; in Article 1, which states the purposes of the United Nations, it is asserted that one of the objectives of the organization is "to develop friendly relations among nations based on respect for the principle of equal rights and self-determination of peoples," a phrase which is repeated in identical form in Article 55. It is in this context of self-determination that the trusteeship system was understood to function.

As in the first period, the concept of self-determination is articulated in universal terms during the post-World War II period, but in practice it is sharply limited and confined. Its application since the Second World War has been almost entirely restricted to the Third World and to the problems of decolonization, and this has meant that the entity to which the principle of self-determination refers has been redefined as well. Instead of the cultural and linguistic communities without political organization which were the subject of discussion after the First World War, it is the politically defined but culturally diverse colonies and ex-colonies of the developing world that have in the latter period structured the debate and shaped the development of the concept. This fact assumes added significance when one considers the status of self-determination in international law, a subject to which we must now turn.

It is important at this point to note the peculiar character of international law as compared to the system of law within sovereign states. Apart from the International Court of Justice, to which states have recourse only with their own consent, there is no agency which in practice is capable of making authoritative judgments about the status of principles or norms of international law or about litigation conducted within its terms. The fact that disputes come before the Court only if the states which are parties to the conflict agree, together with the fact that there is no international police force to enforce the Court's decisions, suggests the degree to which even valid international laws are closer in character to principles of conduct than to binding and compulsory rules. Thus there is a marked tendency for disputes in the international sphere to be settled empirically in each case, even though they may quite clearly involve international legal principles.

The United Nations has been of pivotal significance in the development and application of the concept of self-determination, and a full consideration of this issue would entail dealing with controversial questions regarding the status of the world organization and its institutions as sources of valid international law. We cannot do more than summarize the situation here, and draw out certain implications for Quebec's position in Canada.

The forum for the struggle against colonialism has been the General Assembly where all U.N. members are represented; and in the course of the first decade and a half or so of the U.N.'s history one can detect a notable rise in the temperature of debate as more and more newly independent countries enter the United Nations and throw their weight in the General Assembly behind the effort to end colonialism. We have noted the relevant parts of the U.N. Charter above; Articles I and

100 NATIONALISM, SELF-DETERMINATION AND QUEBEC

55 were appealed to repeatedly in support of anti-colonial arguments. So far as documents specifically relating to human rights are concerned, the Universal Declaration of Human Rights, which was proclaimed by the General Assembly in December 1948, makes no mention of the principle of self-determination, although the International Covenant on Civil and Political Rights and the International Covenant on Economic, Social and Cultural Rights, both adopted by the General Assembly in December 1966, contain identical clauses which read as follows:

> Article 1 (1). All peoples have the right of self-determination. By virtue of that right they freely determine their political status and freely pursue their economic, social and cultural development.

> Article 1 (3). The States Parties to the present covenant, including those having responsibility for the administration of Non-Self-Governing and Trust Territories, shall promote the realization of the right of self-determination, and shall respect that right, in conformity with the provisions of the Charter of the United Nations.

However, these covenants have not been ratified by the necessary two-thirds of member states, leaving them inoperative so far as international law is concerned.

As for the development of attitudes to self-determination within the continuing work of the United Nations, there were throughout the 1950s a series of resolutions reaffirming the right of colonial peoples to independence, calling on administering authorities of trust and non-self-governing territories for reports of progress and estimates of the expected dates of independence, defining the conditions necessary for fulfilling the requirements of self-government and independence, and so forth.[27] But the watershed event in this process was the adoption by the General Assembly in December 1960 of the Declaration on the Granting of Independence to Colonial Countries and Peoples. It enunciated yet again the right of "all peoples" to self-determination and went on to declare that the "inadequacy of political, economic, social or educational preparedness should never serve as a pretext for delaying independence," that all armed action or repressive measures should cease, and that "immediate steps should be taken" in all dependent territories "to transfer all powers to the peoples of those Territories, without any conditions or reservations and without any distinction." What it amounted to was an uncompromising cry to "end colonialism now," and it constituted a clear rejection of the lingering paternalist elements of the U.N. Charter's provision for dealing with dependent territories and peoples. The resolution was adopted unanimously, but significantly nine states, including the U.S., Great Britain, France, Portugal and Australia abstained from the vote. Equally significant, however, is the fact that the decade of the '60s was the period of most intense activity in the field of decolonization, and the declaration provided a focal point for the annual discussion of the degree of progress made in decolonization. Indeed, in the following year a special committee was established to supervise the application of the declaration.

It is within this framework of United Nations' activity that the discussion of the principle of self-determination in international law has been carried on and I think it is fair to say that there is no agreement among the experts as to its status. As early as 1963 one authority in the field concluded that self-determination had developed into an international legal right although its scope and extent were said to be still open to some debate,[28] and many writers can be found who agree with that view. There are others, however, who contend that, while self-determination is undeniably a *principle* of great importance in international affairs, it does not possess or has not yet achieved a formal status in international law.[29] Despite the ambivalent nature of the situation, we have discovered enough to permit us to arrive at a conclusion so far as our concern with Canadian public affairs is concerned.

First of all, we have suggested that there is no consensus of expert opinion about the status of self-determination in international law, although it is conceivable that an exhaustive survey of the literature might indicate that increasingly the weight of judgment is on the side of accepting it as a valid legal rule. Secondly, in our description of the context in which the debate is carried on we have established clearly the cases to which the principle currently applies, namely, colonial or dependent territories. Despite the universal language in which the principle is couched, even those who claim that self-determination is a valid legal rule do not see it as applying to cases other than those involving decolonization. Thus, the right of self-determination, if it exists, means in substance the right of colonial peoples to shed the bonds of empire and to accede to independence. There is little if any disagreement about that.

This is a significant finding from our point of view because it provides conclusive evidence that, even on the assumption that a legal right of self-determination does exist, it does not apply to such a case as Quebec in the Canadian federal structure. Another way of putting this is to say that self-determination has not been interpreted to include the right of secession or of revolution; decolonization in this respect has been viewed, not as secession, but as the "restoration" of sovereignty to the legitimate possessors, the colonial peoples themselves.[30] Indeed, the newly independent countries have been decidedly hard-nosed on the question of secession, and for a very good reason: even more than most of the older political communities, the states of the Third World face the serious and continuing threat of fragmentation and collapse as the cultural and ethnic identities which are not reflected in the political frontiers reassert themselves in the post-independence era. It is therefore not surprising that leaders of these new regimes are desperately concerned to argue that self-determination can be employed once in the process of securing independence from the imperial power, but that it cannot be resorted to subsequently in order to achieve the political reorganization or break-up of the country. Such fragile communities cannot afford to be other than scrupulous in supporting the principles of domestic jurisdiction and non-intervention by foreign powers.

An October 1970 General Assembly Declaration on Principles of International Law concerning Friendly Relations and Co-operation among States puts the point with utmost clarity. After rehearsing in detail the provisions relating to self-determination, the declaration concludes: "Nothing in the foregoing paragraphs shall be construed as authorizing or encouraging any action which would dismember or impair, totally or in part, the territorial integrity or political unity of sovereign and independent States conducting themselves in compliance with the principle of equal rights and self-determination of peoples as described above and thus possessed of a government representing the whole people belonging to the territory without distinction as to race, creed or colour." And then, as if to clinch the matter, the declaration concludes by repeating: "Every State shall refrain from any action aimed at the partial or total disruption of the national unity and territorial integrity of any other State or country."[31]

It may be that with the passing of the postwar wave of decolonization we are on the brink of a new phase in the continuing story of self-determination. If that is so, it seems likely that the cases which will occupy the attention of the world and of international lawyers in the future will be much closer in character and incidence to the case of Quebec; that is to say, it seems probable that many of the future occasions in which a right of self-determination is claimed will involve the attempted secession of a region or national minority from an existent sovereign state.[32] Omens of the future may be found in the unsuccessful secessionist movement of the Ibos in Nigeria and the successful drive to independence of Bangladesh. In neither case can one discover much ground for optimism about the maturity and humanity with which such critical struggles will be handled, nor much reason to hope that the norms and practices of international law and diplomacy will be significant moderating influences in the resolution of conflict of this sort.

Indeed, the two cases of Biafra and Bangladesh seem to lend support to the assertion we made above, that, because of the acute limitations of international law, disputes and conflict will typically be settled according to the circumstances of each case, and not normally by external arbitration and the application of general principles of international law and justice. In geopolitical terms there was a crucial difference between Biafra and Bangladesh, which goes some way toward explaining why one secessionist movement failed and the other succeeded. Biafra was an integral part of the territory of Nigeria and was unable to secure any significant assistance from major foreign powers; Bangladesh, on the other hand, was separated from West Pakistan by a thousand miles and India, which lay between the two parts of the country, saw its own interests engaged in the Pakistani civil war and was in fact hostile to West Pakistan. Thus it was an impossible military situation for West Pakistan. One wonders what might have happened in the Nigerian conflict if one or more of the major powers had thrown their support solidly behind Biafra.

It seems fair to say that this type of case presents difficulties and challenges of an altogether different order compared to the cases of decolonization which we have been considering in the latter part of this chapter. If the three decades of decolonization since the war have not served to make the status of self-determination clear, it is doubtful that a period characterized by secessionist struggles and civil wars will do much to clarify the situation. Should the cause of self-determination be advanced in these circumstances, every state is likely to be the loser and so long as the sovereign state dominates the world political scene one can expect that such an explosive principle as self-determination will be held tightly in rein. Prime Minister Trudeau very clearly viewed the thing as political dynamite in the case of Nigeria, a federal country which, like Canada, is marked by pronounced cultural diversity, and he was scrupulous to ensure that the Canadian government's position could in no way be construed as lending support or tacit approval to Biafra.

What all this seems to suggest is that there is little assistance to be looked for in the realm of international law in working out the relationship between the two communities in Canada. The status of self-determination is unclear, but even if it could be established as a valid rule of international law it would not in its present form be applicable to Quebec. If there is any overall judgment one can make, it is that there is no sanction within the canons of international law for secession. Let us turn directly to Canada now.

NOTES

1. Quoted in Robert Randle, "From National Self-Determination to National Self-Development," *Journal of the History of Ideas,*

Self-Determination in International Relations   105

vol. 31 (1970), p. 61, whose article was helpful in the preparation of this paragraph.

2. See Rupert Emerson's discussion of this point in "Self-Determination," *American Journal of International Law*, vol. 65 (1971), pp. 462-3.

3. *The Political Thought of Woodrow Wilson*, ed. E. David Cronon (New York: Bobbs-Merrill, 1965), p. 422.

4. Ibid., p. 413.

5. Ibid., p. 403.

6. Ibid., p. 346.

7. Ibid., p. 299.

8. Gary Wills, *Nixon Agonistes* (Signet Books, 1971), p. 396.

9. *The Political Thought of Woodrow Wilson*, p. 283.

10. Ibid., p. 343.

11. Ibid., p. 337.

12. Ibid., p. 347.

13. Ibid., p. 445. The address which includes the Fourteen Points and the subsequent address setting out the four supplementary points appear on pp. 438-50.

14. Quoted in A. B. C. Cobban, *The Nation State and National Self-Determination* (London: Collins, 1969), p. 66. I am much indebted to Cobban's study in the first part of this chapter.

15. Ibid., p. 66.

16. Ibid.

17. Barbara Tuchman, in *Stilwell and the American Experience in China: 1911-1945* (New York: Bantam Books, 1972), pp. 72-5, describes the expectations aroused in China by President Wilson's wartime statements and their subsequent bitter disappointment at the peace conference.

18. Cobban discusses the use of plebiscites in *The Nation State*, pp. 70-3, and notes that they were resorted to much less frequently than one might have expected: "in general the opposition to the plebiscitary mode of determining the future of communities came from the victorious Allies, especially from the lesser states, while the demand for plebiscites was a defensive weapon employed by the defeated powers." Cobban concludes that the simplest explanation of the situation would be that "each side was prepared to appeal to the principle when it assisted in the defence of national interests, and to discard it when its influence was no longer favourable." He adds, however, that most of the leading politicians accepted the view that a variety of factors would have to be taken into account. (See as well S. Wambaugh, *Plebiscites Since the World War*, 1933.)

19. H. A. L. Fisher, *A History of Europe*, p. 1161.

20. F. P. Walters in *A History of the League of Nations* (London: Oxford University Press, 1952) gives a useful account of the League, and in chapters 1-4 he describes the gradual emergence to prominence of the League idea prior to its actual creation.

21. Ibid., p. 31.
22. The Covenant is reproduced in chapter 5 of Walters. It appears as well as an appendix to the Goodrich and Hambro edition of the U.N. Charter, cited below.
23. *On Liberty,* chapter 1. See also *Representative Government,* chapter 2.
24. Cited in Randle, "From National Self-Determination to National Self-Development," p. 65, where this case is discussed. See also Walters, *History of the League,* pp. 103-5.
25. The Atlantic Charter, 14 August 1941, for example, asserted as one of the common principles of Britain and the United States "the right of all peoples to choose the form of government under which they will live." Barbara Tuchman, however, in *Stilwell and the American Experience in China,* documents the tensions characterizing the wartime policy-making of Britain and the U.S. in Asia, which were related in part to the incompatability of British imperial interests in the area and American democratic and republican ideals.
26. See the discussion in L. M. Goodrich, Edvard Hambro and A. P. Simons, eds., *Charter of the United Nations: Commentary and Documents,* third and revised edition (New York: Columbia University Press, 1969), pp. 469ff.
27. A useful summary of U.N. experience in this area up to 1971 may be found in the Economic and Social Council (ECOSOC) report, "Implementation of United Nations Resolutions relating to the Right of Peoples under Colonial and Alien Domination to Self-Determination" (E/CN.4/1081), 4 February 1972, (hereafter referred to as ECOSOC *Report*). Excerpts from the relevant U.N. declarations, covenants and resolutions are cited in this report.
28. Rosalyn Higgins, *The Development of International Law Through the Political Organs of the United Nations* (London: Oxford University Press, 1963), p. 103.
29. For a useful discussion of the state of opinion in this matter, see Rupert Emerson, "Self-Determination," *American Journal of International Law,* vol. 65 (1971), pp. 459-75.
30. See Emerson, "Self-Determination," p. 465.
31. ECOSOC *Report,* p. 24.
32. Some scholarly discussion of this matter in the context of international law is currently going on. See, for example; Ved P. Nanda, "Self-Determination in International Law: the Tragic Tale of Two Cities — Islamabad (West Pakistan) and Dacca (East Pakistan)," *The American Journal of International Law,* vol. 66 (1972), pp. 321-36; S. Prakash Sinha, "Is Self-Determination Passé?," *Columbia Journal of Transnational Law,* vol. 12 no. 2 (1972), pp. 260-73.

7.   Federalism and
        Self-Determination

Federalism is a device designed to cope with the problem of how distinct communities can live a common life together without ceasing to be distinct communities. In a sense, it can be regarded as an attempt to reconcile the often conflicting impulses of self-determination and association; the distinct units or communities which together compose the federation are presumed to possess the liberty to pursue their own development in their own sovereign domain on the condition that they agree to forego the unilateral pursuit of their interests in areas of joint enterprise or overlapping purpose.

We mentioned earlier the social-contract model which many seventeenth- and eighteenth-century liberal theorists employed to articulate their belief that the basis of political society was individual consent. A contractual model is illuminating in understanding federalism as well, and it is often in fact a fairly close approximation to the facts; the main difference is that the contracting parties which agree to associate with one another are not individuals, but social collectivities. Very often such groups do actually exist prior to the creation of a federal system, as in the case of the Thirteen Colonies in America and the four British North American colonies which formed the Canadian Confederation.[1] But even where there are not already communities in existence, as in the case of the necessarily arbitrary creation of North and South Dakota and Saskatchewan and Alberta, the assumption is that there are purposes which can best be served on a regional rather than a national basis and that local institutions and loyalties will in time emerge. This has in fact occurred in the case of Alberta and Saskatchewan which in a very short space of time have produced distinct political cultures and in many ways distinguishable patterns of economic and social life.

Federalism is a supremely difficult form of government to operate. It is not so difficult to create; the problem is in sustaining it. One of two impulses generally prevails in the long run: the pull of the centrifugal forces which lead in the direction of disintegration; or the pull of the integrating forces which move the country towards an increasingly centralized form of government. One might say that the health of a federation *as a federation* depends on the interplay and balance of these two opposing forces. In the abstract, federalism is the obvious form of political organization for many regions of the world, and a wide range of federal experiments have been undertaken since the United States first introduced the system into the modern world in 1787. On the gloomy side, we have seen since the Second World War both the creation and collapse of such federal states as Pakistan, Rhodesia and Nyasaland, and the West Indies Federation, and we have witnessed the expulsion of Singapore from the Federation of Malaysia in 1965 and a bloody civil war in Nigeria after Biafra's attempted secession in 1966. On the other hand, as R. L. Watts points out, four of the longest-lasting constitutional systems in the world today are federal: the federal constitution of the United States was adopted in 1787, Switzerland's in 1848, Canada's in 1867 and Australia's in 1900.[2]

However, Watts is also constrained to note that the United States experienced a civil war in 1861-65; that for five centuries the Swiss confederacies were engaged in intermittent military struggle and that the present constitution was adopted after a civil war in 1847 in which federal forces crushed a rebellion by a separatist league of seven cantons called the Sonderbund; and finally that Australia faced and surmounted an independence movement in Western Australia which culminated in a 1933 referendum when the citizens of that state voted for secession.

The reasons why the odds seem to be against the survival or continuance of a political system in genuinely federal form are obvious. Although members of federations often come to appreciate and value the political system in which they live, the initial choice of a federal form of government is almost always a second-best proposition. It is settled upon because, for any of a variety of reasons, a unitary form of government will not work; the reasons may be size, geographical division, cultural, linguistic or religious diversity, distinct social and political traditions, economic specialization, or any combination of these, but it is invariably a matter of working out a basis of association for a new country which lacks certain vitally important "natural" forces of integration. This means that a federal citizen's commitment and loyalty must be to a political and constitutional order without the added support of customs and affections which could serve to tie the federal community together.

Federalism, then, is a political form which is always vulnerable to secessionist movements and disintegration, for it is by explicit design an institutional expression within the political structure itself of the diversity which characterizes the associated communities. The commitment to the federal regime is commonly based on a rational calculation of the needs and interests of one's own community, and a judgment that they are best served by an association with other groups. Therefore, reasons can generally be given for membership in a federal political system, even if it is nothing more glorified than the argument that we will all hang separately if we don't hang together. But very often reasons cannot be given for membership in the basic communities out of which a federal system is constructed, at least not in the same sense; for example, one does not normally think of giving a reason for being a French Canadian, but it is perfectly possible to give a reason or reasons for Quebec's membership in Confederation.

Canadian federalism has on balance worked very well in the sense that the country has so far resisted both the sweep of relentless centralization and the centrifugal force of uncompromising regionalism and separation. Since 1867 there have been long periods of centralization, but not without counteracting trends in which the provinces have vigorously asserted their rights and autonomy. Indeed, today some fear that federalism in Canada has worked rather too well, for there is no denying the diversity of the country and the vigour and energy of the provinces as regional concentrations of political power. Many writers have noted the ironic fact that the United

States, which started out with a constitution favouring the states rather than the federal government, has become (admittedly after a civil war) more and more centralized, while Canada, having apparently learned its lesson from observing American federalism, began with a system favouring a strong central government and yet now in the 1960s and 1970s faces an acute and potentially disastrous provincial challenge to federal power—and not only from Quebec.

No one would suggest that the federal constitution has been the sole factor responsible for the continuing pluralism of Canadian society. The size and sparse population of the country have been factors of considerable importance. And the dominant sociological fact which gave rise to a federal system in the first place, rather than the "legislative union" which Macdonald and others would have preferred, has continued to exercise its effects. The existence of the French-Canadian community in British North America, and the unwillingness or inability of either the imperial authorities or the colonial majority to impose a settlement regardless of the will of the minority, have been of crucial importance in sustaining the diversity upon which federal government rests.

Indeed, they helped to keep alive possibilities which only very recently have been taken up and recognized in any formal, public way in Canada. It seems fair to say that in the nineteenth century, while the French, English, Irish and Scottish were to some extent recognized as distinct cultural groups, the major social cleavages were to be found in the criss-crossing distinctions that were made between the British and the French and between Catholics and Protestants. Linguistically, concern was restricted to French and English in recognition of the fact that, while there might be a degree of ethnic and cultural diversity within the British community, there was nevertheless linguistic unity.

With the successive waves of non-British immigration which began during the premiership of Laurier and which have continued throughout the twentieth century, a new problem and a new set of possibilities arose. Instead of a social ethic which was predominantly dualist, the serious possibility of a multicultural society appeared. The existence in Canada of a large and coherent French-Canadian minority kept open, in a way that was not true of the United States, the possibility of third and fourth cultures flourishing and perhaps even receiving institutional recognition. The term "mosaic" was apparently first used to describe Canadian society in a book on the Canadian West which was published in 1922; the cultural mix and variety of western Canada was called "a mosaic of vast dimensions and great breadth."[3] Both the date of first use and the geographical area of Canada to which the concept was applied are illuminating of that period of immigration and settlement.

Despite French Canada's role as an unconscious guarantor of cultural pluralism, it must be said that the French-Canadian community has been inclined to view the claims of third cultures and languages as a threat, on the grounds that any full-scale acceptance of the ideal of multiculturalism will lead to the practical diminution of the importance of the French fact; French Canada may come to be regarded as one of a number of minority cultures in a predominantly Anglo-Saxon or at least English-speaking country. As one would expect, just the reverse set of attitudes has held true for the non-French and non-British cultural groups; however much the Ukrainians or the Germans or the Italians may in fact owe to the French Canadians for sustaining the ideal of cultural pluralism in Canada, representatives of these cultural minorities perceive the institutional acceptance of dualism, of biculturalism and bilingualism, as a serious obstacle in the way of their interests and aspirations. To the extent that dualism becomes the dominant norm, the focus of attention is directed towards the two dominant communities and languages, with the danger that the other cultural groups may disappear from public view.

These cross-cutting pressures were acutely felt and often forcefully expressed in the work of the Royal Commission on Bilingualism and Biculturalism during the 1960s. The commission's terms of reference made ambiguous use of both concepts, dualism and multiculturalism, although they gave primacy to the former. The commissioners were directed "to inquire into and report upon the existing state of bilingualism and biculturalism in Canada and to recommend what steps should be taken to develop the Canadian Confederation on the basis of an equal partnership between the two founding races, taking into account the contribution made by the other ethnic groups to the culturalism enrichment of Canada and the measures that should be taken to safeguard that contribution." Representatives of both "the two founding races" and "the other ethnic groups" were appointed as commissioners and were active as well in the administrative and research functions of the commission, and of course both elements of Canadian society were dealt with in the commission's *Report* and in its publications of research findings.

Simultaneously with the recent flowering of French language and culture in Canada and the increased awareness throughout the country of the so-called French fact there has been a growing acceptance of the implications of the idea of a Canadian mosaic. There have been, for example, some signs recently that the special claims and problems of the native communities in Canada, the literal "founding races," may receive more adequate recognition, especially by the federal government. Also, we have seen the establishment of a ministry of state for multiculturalism within the federal government, the relaxation by some provinces of school regulations to permit educational instruction in languages other than English or French, and such state-supported celebrations of diversity as Heritage Ontario in 1972. Such things as these indicate that multiculturalism has become part of the conventional wisdom and an accepted social ideal for many Canadians. How such an ideal can be worked into the institutional fabric of the country and related to the concept of dualism and to the regional differentiation which marks the Canadian experience is a matter of considerable importance and complexity.

Since the mid-nineteenth century when Confederation was in the making, there has been a vast increase in the range and variety of activities in which a government is expected directly to participate.[4] This has subjected representative institutions and traditional cultures and patterns of authority to intense stress in many countries, and Canada is no exception in this regard. Not only have Canadians been engaged in building a community and a political order, but the conventional understanding of what a community is, of the division between the public and the private realm, of the proper scope of collective action to mitigate social ills, has been changing rapidly as the work goes on. Thus Canadians during the last century have been engaged, not only in creating a system of government, but also in defining and re-defining and defining yet again what that government can legitimately be expected to do. For example, when the Fathers of Confederation allocated such areas of responsibility as education, municipal institutions, health and social welfare to the exclusive jurisdiction of the provinces, they can have had no inkling of the explosion of activity that would occur in these fields during the next five generations.

There are two broad trends which have converged in Canada in recent years, and which help to encourage the tensions and divisive forces which mark Canadian society today. The first is the increase in the responsibilities and powers of governments in general, whether they be federal, provincial or municipal, an increase which issues out of the growing complexity of the social order and the interdependence between individuals and groups which characterizes modern society itself. The second is the marked increase in Canada in the power of the provincial governments relative to that of the federal government. This second trend (or, more accurately, the current phase of provincial assertiveness) is a quite recent thing, which began to develop in the early 1960s and which has been gathering strength ever since.

The broadening scope of governmental activity is a worldwide phenomenon, but it is one from which Quebec stood apart as much as it could and for as long as it could. The provincial jurisdiction, within which French Canadians constituted a clear majority, has always been the one upon which French Canada as a collectivity could rely, and for much of the Confederation period the accepted patterns of thought in French Canada led naturally to the belief in a minimal role for the state. Political affairs, and to a great extent commercial and industrial life, were hived off as much as possible from the ongoing life of French Canada, as the focus of attention was concentrated upon the maintenance of a culture which did not depend on the fearsome complexities of factory and metropolis, but on the simpler ways of parish and village and farm.

If it is not misleading to describe the general direction and modes of action of a culture as a "strategy," one can say with the benefit of hindsight that this strategy was doomed to fail, especially since it was pursued within the context of a larger society, for the down-playing and ignoring and denying of activities and attitudes alien to the traditional culture did not make them disappear. At best it retarded a process of modernization and development which was continuing regardless. At worst it denied an entire culture the opportunity of gradually assimilating the forces of change and reconciling them with its own habits and outlook, of impressing its own needs and values on the innovation rather than suffering the imposition of alien values which were an inevitable part of the process of innovation when the source of its dynamism lay outside the indigenous culture.

Politically, this meant two things: first, that French Canadians were not moved in large numbers to participate in the political affairs of the country as a whole; and second, that they were not as a community disposed to exploit fully the possibilities which majority control of provincial jurisdiction offered them, but were in the main content to employ the instruments of the state to *resist* change rather than control it. The effect of this was that the English-speaking community which was in the majority at the federal level was pretty much able to have its own way, even with regard to the clash of cultures outside of Quebec; and, while it could obviously not dominate the provincial government in Quebec, it found the French-Canadian ideology of withdrawal and non-participation a perfect adjunct to its own commercial and industrial ambitions in the province. Anglo-Saxon entrepreneurs were perfectly content to allow the leaders of French Canada to attend to the affairs of God, so long as they were permitted to attend to the affairs of men.

This arrangement did not suit the federal government badly either, since, with the exception of certain sacrosanct areas, it granted to the central power a wide freedom of action. The balance of power between the federal government and the provinces has swung back and forth in Canadian history, but for the better part of this century the dominant trend has been that of centralization. Two world wars and an economic depression provided the circumstances in which the emergency and residual powers of the federal government could be employed, and they permitted the federal legislature and civil service to seize and keep the initiative until quite recently.

Students of Canadian federalism writing in, say, 1955 could have been forgiven for believing that the Canadian federal system would continue to develop along lines parallel to the American, which is to say, an attenuation of the power of the regional governments relative to that of the central government. For a decade and a half after the Second World War the Canadian government exhibited a confidence and energy, and a willingness to assume new and complex responsibilities, which placed the provinces very much in the shadow. However, in the early '60s the tide began to turn. The newly elected Lesage government in Quebec led the attack but was joined by a number of other provinces, for although many of its concerns were peculiar to itself, it shared a number of grievances with the wealthier provinces of Ontario, Alberta and British Columbia. What Quebec had in common with them was a growing desire to assume or regain control over a wide range of social-policy matters which fell within provincial jurisdiction and a belief that Ottawa ought to vacate certain tax fields and give up certain revenue sources to the provinces so that they could afford to do the jobs they wanted to do themselves. From 1962 to 1968 a minority Conservative or Liberal government in Ottawa faced powerful provincial politicians and increasingly skilled and sophisticated provincial civil servants; and while it is difficult to assess the precise consequences of this, it is nevertheless reasonable to conclude that the existence of a sometimes demoralized and always vulnerable federal government gave breathing space in which the self-confidence of the provinces could develop. In any case, with provincial premiers as powerful and secure as Bennett, Manning, Robarts and Lesage then were, it is doubtful that conflict and adjustment could have been avoided even by a majority government in Ottawa.

While Quebec had a number of important interests in common with these provinces, its overall position and problems were nevertheless unique. The 1960 Quebec provincial election in which Jean Lesage's Liberal party turned out the Union

Nationale after a generation of political rule is rightly regarded as a watershed event in recent Quebec political history. This marked the beginning of the so-called Quiet Revolution and led very rapidly to the most serious challenge to Canadian federalism since its inception in 1867. The Royal Commission on Bilingualism and Biculturalism presented a *Preliminary Report* early in 1965 and in the preamble the commissioners, in a famous statement, indicated that their initial enquiries had driven them to the conclusion "that Canada, without being fully conscious of the fact, is passing through the greatest crisis in its history." The crisis has increased in its seriousness and proportions since that was written, but the consciousness of the crisis, at least outside of Quebec itself, has not caught up or even kept pace. The commissioners went on to state concisely what they took to be the character of the problem: "the state of affairs established in 1867, and never seriously challenged, is now for the first time being rejected by the French Canadians of Quebec."

This statement properly locates the source of the tensions as they manifested themselves in the early '60s: a change in the character and aspirations of French-Canadian society itself. From the beginning of this period, the rest of the country, which was not itself the source of the dynamic of change, found itself in a defensive posture reacting to the criticisms and demands and proposals of a society which was experiencing a period of rapid transformation. It was fashionable in those days to ask what Quebec wanted, although this sounds quaint today. The underlying idea was that, with good or ill grace, if English-speaking Canadians could only find out what Quebec wanted of them, then the reasonableness of the request could be considered and in all likelihood an accommodation could be made. This was the period when the images of a Canadian "family" and an English and French-speaking "marriage" were popular, with Quebec typically cast in the role of a demanding wife. But whatever limited utility this approach to the issue may seem to have had at the beginning of the Quiet Revolution, it is evident today that it misses the main point; for it has become clear that Quebec increasingly is not as much concerned directly with the relations with the rest of Canada, but much more with its own character and identity, with working out and resolving its collective destiny. It is tacitly assumed by many Quebeckers that if this can be done satisfactorily, then the proper relationship of Quebec to the rest of Canada, but not just to the rest of Canada, to North America as a whole and to the rest of the world, will then become apparent. The complex challenge as it presents itself to the *Québécois* is one of determining autonomously what social, economic and cultural arrangements will best serve to fulfill the aspirations of the whole community. In meeting this challenge, Quebec regards the rest of the country as an onlooker, rather than as a participant. This is not to say that Quebec's relationship with Ottawa and the other provinces is not important; obviously it is. But it is to suggest that for growing numbers of *Québécois* the primary issue is not Quebec's position in Canadian federalism itself, but rather the resolution by Quebeckers of the kind of society they want Quebec to be.

Many writers have attempted to characterize the way in which Quebec of the '60s and '70s differs from what went before. A favourite technique has been to concentrate on French Canada's perception of its task in North America and to argue that a strategy of *survivance* has been replaced by an energetic and effervescent *épanouissement*, that the minimal desire for survival has been supplanted by a demand that French-Canadian society be permitted to blossom, to expand and develop. This is no doubt a useful formula and it is particularly helpful from the point of view of our concern with nationalism, because it focuses attention on the collective consciousness of French-Canadian society.

Léon Dion and others spoke in the early 1960s of a "nationalism of growth," and the affinity between growth and *épanouissement* (literally, "blooming," "blossoming") is obvious. However, Dion complicates the picture in an article which appeared in the *Canadian Forum* in January 1964 when he points out that in Quebec's recent history there has been "a depression nationalism, a wartime nationalism, a nationalism of prosperity and finally, in the present decade, a nationalism of growth." In one sense this is perfectly true, and it draws our attention once again to the fact that nationalism is contextual, that it depends for its specific content upon the historical environment in which it exists. Thus it can be shown that the visage of French-Canadian nationalism has altered according to whether it is confronting the problems of economic depression and dislocation, the mobilization for war and conscription, or a postwar period of economic expansion and the concomitant self-confidence of an aggressive federal government.

However, in the light of our particular interest, it can be seen that Dion's typology is quite seriously misleading in another respect, for what it calls attention to are the *problems* with which French Canada was preoccupied, rather than the *strategy* it employed to cope with them. When we consider the question of strategy or the spirit which animates French-Canadian nationalism, we can see that the so-called nationalism of growth is distinct from all the other forms which Dion mentions, and that the *survivance-épanouissement* dichotomy illuminates this much more clearly.

At the risk of drastic over-simplification, the transformation of Quebec which is symbolized by the electoral victory of the Lesage Liberals in 1960 might be stated in the form of a paradox. Throughout its entire history French Canada's paramount objective as a community has been to preserve itself; this is as true today as it was in 1760. However, prior to 1960 self-preservation meant resistance to change, keeping apart from external influences that would threaten to alter the composition of French-Canadian society. After 1960, self-preservation meant the acceptance, even the welcoming, of change, for it was realized that if French Canada were to stay the same everything had to be altered. If French Canada was to preserve itself it had to take control of its destiny and become the initiator of change rather than the subject of innovations that were determined elsewhere. This altered consciousness has, I think, grown out of the realization that in the twentieth century no community can hope to sustain itself for long in isolation and immobility, but must seek its security rather in the dynamic pursuit of its own good and in the progressive development of its identity—in short, in the expression of a spirit of *épanouissement* or a nationalism of growth.

This account, brief as it is, nevertheless seems to me to indicate the quality of the change that Quebec society has undergone in the past few years. Clearly, it has been vastly more complicated than a short sketch can suggest, and it is evident as well that any investigation of the process will quickly uncover a whole range of economic, religious, social and cultural factors, intricately interrelated with one another and extending well back into Quebec history. But such a summary does serve to draw our attention to the fact that not just the tasks of politics, but the context or atmosphere in which politics is conducted has been drastically altered, and altered in such a manner that no party or politician aspiring to office can fail to heed the distinctive way in which contemporary problems are expressed and approached in Quebec society. Ever since the Liberals campaigned in 1960 on a platform of *maîtres chez nous,* which must surely have been the most successful slogan in Canadian politics in the '60s, the nationalist verities that had stood Quebec in good stead for generations have been crumbling away, and public figures have had to learn to recognize a new set of political fault lines and nationalist landmarks.

Nineteen sixty, then, marks the beginning of a new period in the history of the French-Canadian community, and the appearance of a discernibly novel attitude to change in Quebec society. It is not so much that a set of radical innovations was introduced all at once, although it is true that quite a number of reforms were instituted in a short space of time; much more important is the innovative, liberating spirit which began to transform Quebec's approach to its affairs. This spirit of liberation, this sense of shrugging off the constraints of religious and social conformity and taking hold of one's fate, is the thread which ties together the apparently disparate events and actions which have marked recent Quebec history. Societies in the grip of rapid transformation are typically characterized by an acute volatility of opinion and by pronounced internal conflict, and Quebec is clearly no exception; but what in the vast majority of cases all parties to the conflict share is an assumption that change in their society is necessary and that improvement and reform are possible. Typically the debates in which politically active Quebeckers participate revolve around reformist and radical strategies of various kinds; they do not, normally, turn on a disagreement about whether change is required at all.[5]

In light of what we have been saying, the origins and main lines of the conflict between French and English Canada should be apparent. As Canadians, we have moved from a situation in which the needs and aspirations of the two communities— and of the provincial and federal governments—were roughly speaking congruent, to a situation in which they are in conflict, and sometimes directly contradictory. During much of our history, what English Canada wanted to do meshed satisfactorily with what French Canada wanted (or did not want) to do. And much the same held true for the two levels of government. However, there have been periods when this has not been so, and the past decade and a half has been marked by the unsettling presence of intersecting and conflicting purposes and by the absence of any authoritative institutions which are recognized as fully legitimate by all sides and within which the tensions can be resolved. Our political experience during the last fifteen years has been characterized by conflict *between* various political institutions rather than by conflict *within* them —by, for example, federal-provincial ministerial meetings, rather than by the clash of parties within Parliament.[6]

We have now experienced a decade of effort directed to working out a satisfactory relationship between Quebec and the rest of Canada, first of all the well-intentioned pragmatism of the Pearson government and then the doctrinaire brinkmanship of Prime Minister Trudeau, and neither has proved to be capable of producing the desired results. The process of constitutional reform, begun under the Pearson administration and continued for three wearing years under the stewardship of Mr. Trudeau, collapsed with Quebec's rejection of the Victoria Charter in June 1971, and until quite recently there has been virtually no interest from any quarter in resuming that vexing task. There was some speculation immediately after the Quebec election of October 1973 about the reopening of constitutional discussion, but Prime Minister Trudeau expressed no great desire to see this occur, saying that he was less enthusiastic than in 1966 about constitutional reform, and indicating that any initiative on this score would have to come from Quebec and offer some real hope of success before the federal government would be justified in taking the matter up again.[7] Given the prime minister's increasing caution and the pragmatism of the current Quebec government, a resumption of serious constitutional discussion at this point would be surprising.

Where large-scale creative efforts have proven unavailing, it may yet be that piecemeal adjustment, assisted by the subtle force of inertia, will win through. This is what many commentators, who have opposed constitutional reform, have been advocating all along. But if we manage to muddle through, I would expect the accommodation to be made more in the field of economic and social policy than directly in the realm of cultural policy. It seems likely that, if a new equilibrium can be achieved, it will involve first and foremost the construction of a satisfactory position for Quebec within the Canadian federal system and only secondarily the creation of satisfactory arrangements for French Canadians within Canadian society as a whole. This is only to express again the opinion that the collective determination of the character and direction of the *Québécois* community itself is the main task in which French Canada is engaged, and that this is only marginally affected by what happens to French-speaking Canadians in the rest of the country.

The leverage which the federal government's policy of bilingualism and biculturalism can exert on the problem in the short run is slight. This is in no sense to deny that there is much to applaud in its commitment to cultural and language policies which are designed to recognize and support the major cultural forces in the country, and to place as far as possible the French and English languages on a footing of equality. These policies can be defended as a matter of justice. However, it is in my opinion unrealistic to think that they can do much directly to effect the reconciliation of the two communities, except in the long run. In the area of language policy, for example, one has only to read the annual reports and statements of the Official Languages Commissioner to realize what an arduous and lengthy task it is to alter the linguistic habits of certain public institutions, let alone the practices and attitudes of an entire country.

Evidence in support of the general point we are seeking to

establish here can be found in the fact that even as this laudable concern for linguistic justice has developed in the country there has been a growing alarm shared by many Quebeckers about the likely future of the French language in the province of Quebec itself. With the drastic fall in the birthrate of French Canadians, so that it is today one of the lowest in the country, and with the continuing propensity of immigrants to Quebec to learn English rather than French, Quebec faces the prospect of a weakening position for French even within the province itself. It is concerns of this sort that have led many French Canadians to advocate unilingual French language policies for the province just as the rest of the country begins to make some effort to increase bilingualism. Thus Canadians may yet witness the irony of a federal government making herculean and impressively expensive[8] efforts to transform the public service and other bodies into bilingual institutions, while at the same time Quebec is engaged in moving the province to an increasingly unilingual (French) position. And yet it is transparently clear that the collective vitality of the French language within its home province is and must surely remain one of the primary legitimate concerns of the Quebec community.

While it is obvious that the federal government and the rest of the country have important roles to play in moderating the structural tensions that currently beset the social and political system, it is also apparent that, given the relatively autonomous dynamic of change operating in Quebec society which we have described in the pages above, the best course for English Canada is to ensure that its own interests are secured and, once this is done, to accept the widest latitude of action for Quebec to work out its own destiny in order to see whether a new equilibrium can be achieved.

NOTES

1. We are not here supporting the "compact theory" of the origins of Canadian federalism, but indicating the presupposition in federal systems that significant subordinate entities do exist and possess collective interests and aspirations which ought to be recognized.

2. R. L. Watts, "The Survival or Disintegration of Federation," in *One Country or Two?*, ed. R. M. Burns (Montreal: McGill-Queen's University Press, 1971), p. 41. See also his study for the Royal Commission on Bilingualism and Biculturalism, *Multicultural Societies and Federalism* (Ottawa: Information Canada, 1970). I am much indebted to Watts' essay and his Royal Commission study for the comparative material on federalism in this chapter.
3. Quoted in Allan Smith, "Metaphor and Nationality in North America, *Canadian Historical Review* (September 1970), p. 259.
4. See Donald V. Smiley's article, "Federalism, Nationalism and the Scope of Public Activity in Canada," in Peter Russell, ed., *Nationalism in Canada* (Toronto: McGraw-Hill, 1966).
5. The Créditistes, however, might be regarded as a party whose primary appeal is still to "old Quebec," which is why the accession of Yvon Dupuis to the provincial leadership was so disruptive.
6. Richard Simeon in his book, *Federal-Provincial Diplomacy* (Toronto: University of Toronto Press, 1972), provides an account of Canadian federalism from this perspective, using models drawn from international relations as explanatory aids.
7. *Le Devoir*, 3 November 1973.
8. In March 1974 it was estimated that the federal government would spend $188 million on bilingualism in the coming fiscal year. (*Globe and Mail*, 1 March 1974).

8.   Nationalism and the Politicians

In the spring of 1972 the lengthy work of a parliamentary committee studying constitutional reform was completed with the release of its *Final Report*—ironically, a year after the abortive federal-provincial conference in Victoria in June 1971 had abruptly halted the formal process of constitutional review. Shortly after the *Report's* publication, a group of about forty English-speaking academics, politicians and civil servants met informally at Queen's University to discuss its proposals. The discussions were amiable and intelligent and, although there was disagreement and debate as the weekend progressed, the affair was conducted for the most part without passion or rancour—as befits consideration of as workaday a document as the British North America Act.

There was, however, one jarring note in this song of sweet reason, which occurred during the examination of Chapter 7 of the *Report* entitled "Self-Determination". Of the thirty-seven chapters that composed the document, this was the only one to cause a perceptible rise in the temperature of debate. Most of the discussion of the *Report* had involved a careful analysis of the various proposals for reform and a cool-headed assessment of their viability and merit; with respect to Chapter 7, however, there was, among those who spoke, a shift from analysis to declaration, often the most forthright declaration of belief about the nature of the country and about whether or not secession was a legitimate topic to place on the agenda of constitutional reform. Members of the committee which produced the *Report* and who were present at the Queen's meetings indicated that the passage on self-determination had been the most difficult section to write, and on the evidence of the dissenting statements that appeared at the time of the *Report's* publication, it was the only major section on which it was impossible to secure agreement within the committee.

This degree of sensitivity to the question is in no way atypical of English Canada. The Toronto *Globe and Mail* editorialized apoplectically on the subject while the committee was still preparing its *Report*: "Canadians will be vastly interested to discover that a joint Senate-Commons committee has been arguing in camera, day after day, over a proposal to give provinces the right to break away from Canada. They will also be stunned and furious at the impertinence of the discussion. What peculiar parliamentarians are these who can even fancy they have a mandate to produce recommendations for the destruction of the country. In secret." The editorial then turned to the question of the committee's mandate to consider the proposal to drop opposition to the idea of special status for Quebec and renounce the use of force to prevent Quebec's separation: "The committee must know that there would be wholesale rejection in Canada of such a recommendation from a handful of politicians who were never given a mandate to inquire into an issue that goes to the heart of Canada's survival."[1]

This is strange indeed. It is a peculiar view of the role of a member of Parliament and an even more peculiar idea of the function of constitutional review. The process of review was begun primarily because of Quebec's dissatisfaction with its position in Confederation, and it was that issue, rather than an amending formula or an entrenched Bill of Rights, which invested the review process with a sense of urgency and high importance. In these circumstances, one would have thought that a committee of Parliament studying the constitution of Canada had a perfect right to consider and make recommendations upon any such matters relating to the political organization of the country. If members of Parliament do not have such a right, then who on earth does? It is worth underlining that the *Globe's* explosion occurred before the committee's *Report* was even completed; the editorial is not attacking a formal recommendation which had actually been made, but rather the fact that such a matter is being discussed at all. This truculent and ostrich-like posture is necessarily barren of any policy consequences, except perhaps the policy not to have a policy, and it is an attitude which appears to be fairly widespread in the country.

That the issue of secession should be the one above all others that strikes most deeply into the hearts of English-speaking Canadians is not surprising. In many other countries debate about self-determination and separation has proven to be the prelude to civil war, and in Canada it involves the disruption of the hopes many people have had for their country and a sense of being forced to embark on a hazardous and uncertain venture at someone else's choice rather than at one's own decision.

To speak of secession, then, is to consider in the most direct and explicit way possible the destruction of Canada, the country which is the homeland of Canadians, and for increasing numbers of English-speaking people the only homeland they possess. French Canadians, even those most strongly and genuinely committed to the Canadian state, have always experienced a double allegiance—to the Canadian political community as a whole and to their own French-Canadian community concentrated in Quebec. Their commitment to Canada (and very often in earlier years to the authority of Great Britain as well) was almost invariably predicated on an assumption that it provided the best framework possible for the protection of a French-speaking North American society. For their part, many English-speaking Canadians, especially those of British origin, filtered their allegiance to Canada through an identification with what they took to be a larger and grander organization, the British Empire, and subsequently the British Commonwealth of Nations. As the power and authority of this type of multiracial organization has dwindled and Canada has grown in maturity and self-confidence, so too the loyalty to the British connection has become increasingly attenuated and the allegiance to Canada has become much more direct and self-sustaining.

In fact, the question of national independence for Quebec arouses the most vigorous and emotional reactions among Canadians, whatever their political persuasion and whatever their linguistic and cultural affiliations may be. The difference between the French-speaking and English-speaking community in this respect is not to be found so much in the degree of passion and conviction which members of the two groups bring to the debate—indeed, the heat is in general more intense in

French Canada. The difference lies rather in the fact that French Canada has had to discuss the matter seriously and extensively, whereas in English Canada the issue has on the whole been sublimated. While it is something which can be counted on to produce intense reactions when it is raised, self-determination, at least in its most dramatic form of secession and sovereign independence, is not an issue which has received sustained and thorough consideration in English Canada. This is unfortunate and may prove to be a costly omission if, as is quite possible, Canada at some time in the future is faced with an independence movement which has come to power in Quebec by the operation of the normal processes of representative democracy. Its cost may be high in any case if it can be shown that an unwillingness to think the problem through to the end has meant the closing down of options without serious assessment of them. If all-consideration of a political problem must be structured in terms of a tacit but predetermined end, the possibilities of creative thought or of moving public discussion into new channels are markedly reduced.

The reasons why there should be such reluctance to let the light in on this question are not difficult to discover. Among federal politicians there is an understandable reluctance to initiate debate on such an explosive matter; Woodrow Wilson's Secretary of State at the end of the First World War is far from being the only public figure to see national self-determination as something which is "loaded with dynamite". First of all, there is the simple question of political survival; political leadership, especially in a democratic country, always involves the business of charting an uneasy course somewhere between what the leader thinks is a desired or inevitable state of affairs and what the public is prepared to accept; no politician worth his salt is going to risk abrading the sentiments and attitudes of his constituents on an extremely tender subject unless he believes he has no other responsible choice. Even a man like Charles de Gaulle, apparently so disdainful of the petty arts of politics, turned his celebrated strength of will to enormous political advantage, but, when the people were against him, never forgot how to beat a strategic retreat.

However, there is a second and much more important issue

than mere political survival which helps to explain the circumspection of politicians in this matter. In our social and political affairs we inhabit an environment which is to a very great extent self-created; that is to say, it is a world which is composed in good measure of our opinions and prejudices and expectations, and it is one, too, in which the steps which we and our fellows take are related very directly to our perception of public opinion and our predictions about how other people will react to what we do.

A concrete example of this general point may be found in the American defence policy of massive nuclear retaliation which was a product of the Dulles years. According to this policy, American and Western security could be assured if potential enemies of the United States realized that any armed aggression against America or its allies would lead to the unleashing of the full military might of the United States. Very clearly, the success of the policy was entirely contingent on its never having to be put into effect; if it failed as a deterrent, it failed utterly, for its implementation would mean global destruction. The whole matter turned, therefore, on what was called its credibility, on whether the enemies of the United States *believed* it or not. In this respect, it did not in the abstract matter a rap whether the warheads aimed at the Soviet Union were filled with sand as long as other countries *believed* that they carried nuclear arms and that the United States was prepared to use them. But, practically speaking, of course, to make the deterrent plausible the United States had to arm its missiles with nuclear warheads. International relations, in fact, provide a particularly dramatic example of the extent to which the political world is constructed, not out of some unvarnished external reality, but out of interlocking *opinions about* reality.

Canadian politicians must be very sensitive to this fact in their approach to French-Canadian nationalism, for to talk seriously, even in hypothetical terms, about the separation of Quebec from the rest of Canada may be to engage in a self-fulfilling prophecy. It may be to affect people's attitudes to the country and to its stability in such a way that separation, by the very fact that it is considered openly in the public realm, becomes more likely. This is undeniably a point of great importance, and it is reasonable to suppose that people in positions of political authority have a particular duty to be careful and precise in their public utterances, and especially sensitive to the consequences of what they say when they are speaking about the unity of the country itself.

However, this rule cuts both ways. There is no escape from responsibility; a public figure is as responsible for his silence as for his speech. It must in principle be admitted, I think, that there is a point beyond which the refusal to open consideration of such a painful and intractable issue may fairly be regarded as an avoidance of the duties of public office rather than as an exercise in restraint and statesmanlike caution. Acceptance of the idea that the initiation of discussion of a matter of public importance may in certain circumstances be irresponsible because it may help to bring on the very thing which is to be avoided includes as a necessary corollary the notion that the continuation of silence in other circumstances may be a serious abdication of responsibility.

While this is clear enough in general terms, no one would deny that in practice the matter is complex and there is a large grey area where it is apparent that either course of action may be pursued with honesty and reason. Many people would argue that Quebec stepped back firmly from the brink in the October 1973 provincial election, and it is certainly true that a period of relative quiescence has followed that event. However, we have gone through periods of relative tranquility before when nationalist issues have ceased for a time to command public attention, and yet it is beyond denial that the strength of the independence forces in the province has grown steadily during the past fifteen years. Indeed, I do not think that the results of the last provincial election are as unambiguous as some people would have us believe. It was just a few years ago that one of the country's most eminent students of federalism, and one moreover who in no way can be considered an alarmist, noted that his preparation of a book on Canadian federalism was halted on two occasions because of his judgment that the federation would not last as long as it would take him to finish the manuscript.[2] There is reason, therefore, to believe that the problems of political leadership that we have discussed above will remain with us for some time to come.

In any case, leading federal politicians have not cloaked

themselves in Olympian silence on the subject of Quebec nationalism, although in some instances it might have been better if they had. The October Crisis of 1970 is a veritable gold-mine of wild and unsubstantiated statements by government leaders, including the prime minister, many of which reveal an astonishing insensitivity to the consequences of official utterances.[3] It is especially in times of crisis, when public opinion is likely to be volatile and information slight and uncertain, that the responsibilities of political leadership must be recognized and observed.

So far as the federal parties themselves are concerned, we have suggested that they have not been able to cope satisfactorily with the upsurge of nationalism in Quebec within the bounds of ordinary political activity, nor have they demonstrated a capacity to engage in the extremely difficult task of analysis, public discussion and education which a more radical approach to the problem would require. Part of this may be owing to the regional character of the federal parties, which tends to promote and reinforce the sectionalism of Canada. The Liberals are strong in central Canada, especially in Quebec, the Créditistes are confined to rural Quebec, the Conservatives have their secure power base in the Maritimes and the West, and the NDP remains, despite its best efforts, an English-Canadian party.

The only party which, given the breadth of its electoral support, might be expected to reflect in its internal composition many of the national and cultural tensions of the country as a whole, and thus perhaps be goaded into creative thought on the issue, is the Liberal party, and for more than five years the Liberals have been in the grip of a deeply flawed anti-nationalist doctrine which has had to face little competition at the federal level and which has demonstrated limited internal capacity for change. Although the failure of the process of constitutional reform and the clear and repeated indications from Quebec that bilingual and bicultural improvements in the federal civil service and outside the province (however meritorious in themselves) are not in any way the central issues for French Canada—although this might lead one to expect that Liberal party policy on the national question might be re-examined, there is little indication to date that this is in fact occurring. That the prime minister could suggest in the autumn of 1972 that he had taken it that the problem of national unity had been settled but that the results of the 30 October federal election showed that it was not, and then repeat this thought at the time of the Western Economic Opportunities Conference in the summer of 1973, indicates how little apparent sensitivity there has been within the upper levels of the federal government to the acute and continuing tensions that exist within the Canadian federal system.

The only federal party which seemed at one point to be on the verge of charting some new territory on this issue (as well as the issue of Canadian economic independence) was the New Democratic Party, prompted by its Quebec provincial wing and by the Waffle group. Prior to the national convention of the NDP in the spring of 1971, the Quebec NDP and the Waffle had worked out a position on Quebec, recognizing its absolute right to self-determination and linking that position to a left-wing social and economic policy. There was a coherent opposition force within the NDP and an institutional focus for the expression of a distinctive view of Canadian federalism, and it seemed for a time that the clash between the Waffle and Quebec NDP on the one hand and the moderate sectors of opinion on the other might produce a distinctive national policy for the party. However, with the defeat of the Quebec resolutions at the convention and the election of an uncompromising David Lewis to the party leadership, together with the subsequent resignation of Raymond Laliberté from the presidency of the Quebec NDP, the debate fizzled out. The disbanding and demoralization of the Waffle, which was begun at the provincial council meeting of the Ontario NDP at Orillia in June 1972 and pretty well completed by the Waffle itself at its London conference that August, appears to have put paid to the possibility of vigorous internal debate on the national question for the time being. Indeed, the conclusion of an article in *Le Devoir*[4] published prior to the 1972 federal election that there is little to choose between Messrs. Trudeau, Stanfield and Lewis so far as their policies regarding Quebec and *autodétermination* is concerned continues to be correct, and in fact can fairly be applied to their policies on French Canada generally.

If it is true that the question of Quebec's relationship with the rest of Canada is very far indeed from being resolved, and that there is no possibility of it being "settled" in a short space of time, our judgment about the state of opinion within the federal parties provides grounds for deep concern. But in fairness to the parties, it must be noted that they not only mould, but also respond to public attitudes, and assessment of their behaviour and policies must include reference to the sociological realities on which the parties necessarily depend. Thus the failure of the federal parties since 1960 to seize opportunities as they presented themselves and to capitalize on what freedom of action there was may very well be related to the state of public opinion with respect to this matter. One of the major functions of political parties, after all, is to get votes, and one plausible explanation of party behaviour can be constructed out of an examination of the citizen body on which their electoral strength must depend. A political party can only reconcile differences that are reconcilable, and it may be that a party which attempts genuinely to combine and resolve in policy the conflicts which increasingly beset relations between French and English-speaking Canada commits itself to collective schizophrenia, never a comfortable psychological condition and not one, moreover, which is likely to recommend itself to the voters. Many Conservatives, for example, believe this is what happened to their party in the 1968 election with its *deux nations* platform, and that this accounted in substantial degree for its lack of success at the polls. Whatever possibility there may have been at the beginning of the Quiet Revolution for the federal government to mediate successfully between French and English Canada and to establish a satisfactory position for Quebec in Canadian federalism, there appears today to be reduced latitude for instituting arrangements which have any prospect of lasting and which satisfy the demands, or are at least within the bounds of tolerance, of each national community.

Much has changed in Quebec society since the beginning of the Quiet Revolution. To see this one has only to compare the journalism and political analysis of the early 1960s with what is being written and said (and assumed) today. Jean Lesage and Eric Kierans and René Lévesque would no doubt have been astonished if in 1960 the events that were to occur during the next decade had been unfolded before their eyes. Consider the evolution of separatist opinion and its reflection in party politics since 1960. When Dr. Marcel Chaput's bestseller, *Pourquoi Je Suis Séparatist,* was published in 1961, it was considered daring and perhaps a little unbalanced politically to be a declared separatist. In the preface to his book, the author admits that many people treat separatists as dreamers, and at a 1962 Laval University conference on Canadian federalism at which he spoke, Chaput, aware of the attitudes of his audience, spent much of his time simply trying to persuade the listeners that separatism was indeed a serious and credible option.[5] All this has long since changed; even the language of separatism has matured and has been made consonant with the thought of those who view a sovereign Quebec as the natural state of affairs and Quebec's continued federal membership as abnormal. "Séparatisme" has become "indépendantisme," suggesting the achievement of full autonomy of a coherent social unit (Quebec), rather than the breaking up or fragmentation of a single country (Canada). And the Rassemblement pour l'Indépendance Nationale (RIN), a movement which in its title was focusing on the accession to independence of the French-Canadian nation, has, together with a number of other independence organizations, been supplanted by the Parti Québécois, a party which in its public persona at least virtually assumes the eventual independence of the province of Quebec and which is as much occupied with setting out what it proposes to do with Quebec's sovereignty, once it is achieved, as it is with achieving it. In the 1970 Quebec election the main campaign slogan of the PQ was not some variant of "Ottawa non," a favourite but negative theme of earlier separatist groups, but simply "Oui"—Yes; and it was the most striking slogan of the entire campaign.[6]

There were a number of peripheral organizations (such as Raoul Roy's l'Action Socialiste pour l'Indépendance du Québec) dedicated to the independence of Quebec which were created at the beginning of the Quiet Revolution.[7] The one which proved to be the most significant was the RIN, founded by Marcel Chaput and some others in September 1960, a few months after the general election which brought the Lesage Liberals to power. It began as a movement of popular education, designed to further among Quebeckers the idea of independence. After considerable internal debate about whether the RIN should become a formal political party and, if so, what its ideology, political program and mode of financing ought to be (a debate which saw the departure of Chaput to form his own organization, Le Parti Républicain du Québec), the RIN was launched as a formal party in March 1963. A year later, in August 1964, there was a split between the right and left wings of the RIN with five rightists leaving the party to form the Regroupement National. This group united with the provincial Ralliement des Créditistes in February 1966 and fought that year's provincial election under the name Ralliement National (RN). The RIN, under the leadership of Pierre Bourgault, also fought the 1966 election, and so for the first time since the Quiet Revolution began there were significant independence parties participating in a general election. The two parties received a total of less than 9 per cent of the popular vote: 3.2 per cent for the RN whose major appeal was in rural Quebec, and 5.5 per cent for the RIN whose main strength was in the urban areas, especially in Montreal. In terms of the normal canons of electoral success this was not a great showing, although the significance of almost one in every ten Quebec voters opting for a separatist party ought not to be lost sight of. Also, while neither party was able to win a single seat, the strength of the RIN in certain traditionally Liberal constituencies was said by many commentators to have cost the Lesage government the election.

When René Lévesque, in the course of a Liberal party congress in October 1967, declared himself in favour of Quebec independence and left the Liberals to form the Mouvement Souveraineté-Association (MSA), the stage was set for the unification of all major independence movements under one banner. The arrangements which were to produce a major new political force in the province were completed in the autumn of 1968, when first the Ralliement National and then the Rassemblement pour l'Indépendance Nationale joined with

Lévesque's MSA to create the new organization, the Parti Québécois.

The appearance of the Parti Québécois in October 1968 with Lévesque as its first president was an event of singular importance in recent Quebec history, and one moreover with deep implications for Canada as a whole. It is a political organization utterly different in character from its *indépendantiste* predecessors; it is incomparably better organized, better financed and better led. Indeed, it is not necessary to restrict the comparison solely to other parties and movements which have shared its conviction about the evils of Canadian federalism. The character and capacities of the PQ were evident in the first campaign which it fought during the April 1970 provincial election, when it won seven seats in the legislature, and almost a quarter of the popular vote, coming second only to the Liberals in the latter and ahead of the Union Nationale and the Créditistes. It was clear then, and has become even clearer since, that in terms of the range and quality of its leadership, the degree to which it has articulated a coherent political program, and the enthusiasm and commitment it can call on from its supporters, the Parti Québécois is a match, and in many respects much more than a match, for the Liberals, the Créditistes and the moribund Union Nationale.

This was demonstrated again in the course of the October 1973 provincial election campaign. The leaders, the party program, the enthusiasm and flair were all there, but in addition there was a cool professionalism and sophistication which had been less evident in the previous contest. It seems to me as well that the Parti Québécois, more effectively than any of its competitors, was able to represent an image of Quebec society and its emerging character which was congruent with the experience of the French-Canadian community during the last thirteen years. There was something more than mere campaign strategy in the way in which the PQ leaders placed their party in a line of evolutionary succession with the reformist elements within successive Quebec governments which had been such important agents of change in the recent history of the province.

An observer writing shortly before the election was called pinpointed, acutely if not without bias, an important difference between the Liberals and the PQ: "as we all know man does not live by equalization payments and capital investment alone. There is the soul which must be nurtured and up to now the PQ more than any other party has managed to distill into a political expression the spiritual meaning of what it is to be Québécois. The Liberal answer to this is the concept of 'cultural sovereignty,' a sort of bastard son of *maîtres chez nous* and a distant relative of *égalité ou indépendance*. It means Maria Chapdelaine can live forever so long as we render to David Rockefeller the things that are Chase Manhattan's."[8]

The sweeping victory of Robert Bourassa's Liberal party, which carried off a staggering 102 of 110 seats in the National Assembly, has been interpreted by many as a decisive victory for federalism; it can as easily be viewed as a setback for the democratic process. Certainly, the evidence flows in a number of different directions.

There can, of course, be no doubt whatever that Premier Bourassa's Liberal government received a most vigorous expression of continued confidence from the province's voters. With a good voter turnout and four well-organized parties in the field, the Liberals increased their share of the popular vote by about 10 percentage points compared with their respectable showing of 45 percent of the popular vote in the 1970 election. This result, after three turbulent years in office and a surprisingly quiet and un-inflammatory campaign, must be regarded by any standards as a considerable achievement.

At the same time, the Parti Québécois increased its share of the popular vote by almost as much as the Liberals, receiving support from about 30 per cent of the electorate in 1973 as compared to 23 per cent in 1970. Both the PQ and the Liberals were able to advance their position substantially because of the collapse of the Union Nationale, which fell from almost 20 per cent of the balloting in 1970 to 5 per cent in 1973. On the reasonable assumption that the overwhelming majority of English-speaking citizens in Quebec voted for the Liberals, it would seem that approximately 38 per cent of the French-speaking population supported the PQ compared with about 46 per cent who backed the Liberals.[9] This is necessarily a rough estimate, but what is important and indisputable is the fact that about two out of every five French-speaking voters chose to support a party which had separation and national independence as the central plank in its platform.

Many observers of Quebec politics concluded that the campaign amounted to a kind of referendum on federalism and independence. To the extent that this is correct, the pattern of popular votes reveals a society which is deeply divided within itself; the substantial English-language population, one must assume, voted on bloc for federalism, while the French-Canadian community split almost down the middle on the question of separation. This is a difficult situation in which to conduct the public business of the province, but nevertheless it remains a fact of life which Quebec and the rest of the country have for the time being to live with.

It seems reasonable to suggest that the difficulties and tensions which the province faces as a result of such a deep division of opinion about vitally important matters will be exacerbated if the system by which political power is allocated is perceived to work markedly in favour of one side in the conflict and to the disadvantage of the other, as is presently the case in Quebec. Many people were concerned after the April 1970 election about the disparity between popular votes and seats in the National Assembly, specifically as it related to the Parti Québécois. In that election the Liberals received well under half the popular vote (less in fact than when they *lost* to the Union Nationale in 1966), but formed the government with two-thirds of the seats, while the PQ, with almost a quarter of the popular vote, got just one-fifteenth of the seats.

Despite the redrawing of the constituency map in the interim, the disparity was much worse in the 1973 election. The Liberals, with about 55 per cent of the vote, took more than 90 per cent of the seats, while the Parti Québécois, which received 30 per cent of the vote, obtained 5 per cent of the seats. The PQ, then, markedly increased its share of the popular vote and yet saw its complement in the legislature reduced by one. Thus a gargantuan Liberal majority of 102 members faces six péquistes and two créditistes in the National Assembly.

This is a disturbing situation whether one opposes or advocates Quebec's separation, for it inevitably calls into question the adequacy and fairness of the political institutions which must be the major instrument in resolving the relations between the two national communities humanely and with justice. We noted in the first chapter that most of us most of the time accept the conventions of our system of electoral representation and the imperfections that go along with it. But institutions function adequately only within certain tolerances, and one may now raise the question of whether Quebec has passed beyond the point at which it is possible satisfactorily to justify the continuation of the existing electoral system unaltered.

In the October 1973 election the combined popular vote of the three opposition parties was 45 per cent and yet each of the party leaders was defeated and together the three parties sent just eight of the possible 110 representatives to Quebec City. The study of the various systems of electoral representation is a highly technical field, and one into which we cannot enter just now; but there are a wide variety of adaptations and arrangements from which to choose, many of which would have the effect of bringing popular vote and party representation more nearly into balance. One wonders whether the time might not be ripe for some careful consideration of reform in this area.

Whatever the merits of such reform, the likelihood of the Quebec Liberals, who are currently the main beneficiaries of the inequities of the existing system, acting to correct some of the problems is slight. One must in fairness admit, however, that the grounds for hesitating to embark on such a course need not be entirely partisan, because there is a legitimate basis for caution in introducing changes of this magnitude into a complex system of representation and there are reasons to be uncertain about the precise effects which such a reform would have.

In his 1964 article in *Canadian Forum,* Léon Dion considered the state of affairs at that time and looked ahead into the future. He declared that he accepted separatism as a serious option, but argued that it had not yet been acclimatized to local conditions:

In order to be usable it needs to be previously filtered and domesticated by a great brain and a great heart that is typically French Canadian, it needs to be fused to our dominant idiosyncracies, and to take shape within the values and norms which inspire and sanction our daily acts, in short, to root itself deeply among the people. Someone asks: does this man exist? That is not the question. The problem is to know if the conjuncture will evolve in such a way that the separatist idea can incarnate itself in a party capable of drawing to it the best men in all sectors of society and of uniting with the people. Among them it would doubtless find someone enjoying a great authority and a great prestige who would lead the party and make it a powerful movement.

The Parti Québécois has fulfilled the conditions set out in this thoughtful and prescient statement. Its leadership is both first-rate and home-grown. The party's leaders are among the most skilful and technically competent public figures in the country, and have all been people of considerable importance in the Quiet Revolution of the 1960s: René Lévesque, one-time journalist and popular television personality who became a prominent minister of national resources (1961-65) and minister of family and social services (1965-66) in the Lesage cabinet; Jacques Parizeau, a well-known and highly respected economist who was an economic adviser to three Quebec premiers (Lesage, Johnson and Bertrand); Claude Morin, deputy minister of federal-provincial and intergovernmental affairs at Quebec City from 1963 to 1971 and as such the principal constitutional adviser to Premiers Lesage, Johnson, Bertrand and Bourassa. These men, who are all well-known outside the province, have invested the independence movement with unprecedented authority and purpose. There are others, such as Jacques-Yvan Morin, Abbé Louis O'Neill, Yves Michaud, Bernard Landry and Pierre Marois, who are perhaps less well-known in English Canada, but significant and respected public figures in Quebec. And, of course, there are the seven PQ members of the last National Assembly, some of whom were not returned in the October 1973 election, who in the course of the past three years welded themselves into a small but powerful opposition force in the legislature.

The party itself is a thoroughly indigenous organization and one which in its policies and operating style is likely to make a strong and familiar appeal to French-Canadian society; in addition, its openness and egalitarianism meets the exigencies of the contemporary political era very well. Given the party's moderate social-democratic ideology, it is tempting and in many ways appropriate to describe the Parti Québécois as French Canada's NDP[10]—except for two things. First of all, there is the obvious and massive point that unlike the NDP the PQ advocates the dismembering of the Canadian state. And secondly, the leadership of the PQ, ironically enough, has had more direct experience of government than has the leadership of the federal NDP.

As the Parti Québécois has become "filtered and domesticated" in the environment of Quebec, so too has the idea of independence as a serious and practicable option for the community. During the 1970 campaign the notion of independence frequently elicited frenzied enthusiasm on the one side and near panic on the other; the 1973 campaign was much quieter, and the question of independence was approached a good deal more temperately by both its adherents and its opponents than it had been in the years previous. There were even reports about the frustration of the English-Canadian community in Montreal, dissatisfied with the Liberals, unable to take the UN and Créditistes seriously, but unable to stomach the separatism of the PQ.[11] Clearly, English-Canadian Quebeckers voted overwhelmingly for the Liberals in the event, but the degree of discontent with the party and the extent to which issues other than independence were reasserting themselves in the minds of some English Canadians were themselves a sign of the times.

The rise of the Parti Québécois has coincided with and has contributed to a profound realignment of political forces in Quebec that is still very much in process. Where these changes will lead it is impossible at this point to say with any confidence, but one might hazard two general comments. First, all the evidence suggests that the venerable Union Nationale is a spent force in the province's politics, although to say this is not to rule out the possibility of a new right-wing political organization emerging out of a coalition of conservative forces in Quebec. Secondly, in any new condition of equilibrium which may eventually emerge, it seems safe to say that the PQ, with its current monopoly not only on the independence issue but also on social-democratic ideology, will be the dominant left-of-centre force in French Canada. It is now the official opposition on the National Assembly and the only serious alternative to the Liberals, and it is not impossible that the staggering majority which the Liberals currently enjoy will turn out to be more of a burden than anything else. Premier Bourassa himself gave some sign that he was sensitive to this possibility when he indicated just after the election that given the results the government would have to make a special effort to listen to the views and attend to the concerns of the large minority of citizens who voted against the Liberals.

Is John Diefenbaker's experience instructive here? In 1958 the Conservatives swept into office with 54 per cent of the popular vote and an unprecedented 208 of 265 seats in the House of Commons; in the next election in 1962 the Conservatives were reduced to a minority-government position and in 1963 they were replaced by the Liberals and have not been in office since. One must in prudence assume that the dangers and responsibilities are at least as great as the pleasures in holding a plenitude of power. In any case, our brief account of the continuing presence and the growing strength of the independence movement in Quebec during the past decade suggests that it would be idle to anticipate its early disappearance from the Canadian political scene.

NOTES

1. *Globe and Mail*, 26 October 1971.
2. Donald V. Smiley in his introduction to *Canada in Question: Federalism in the Seventies* (Toronto: McGraw-Hill Ryerson, 1972).
3. Denis Smith examines many of these in *Bleeding Hearts . . . Bleeding Country* (Edmonton: M.G. Hurtig, 1971).
4. 21 September 1972.
5. *Le Canada, expérience ratée . . . ou réussie?/The Canadian Experiment, Success or Failure?* (Quebec City: Les Presses de l'Université Laval, 1962).

6. A point made in a *Last Post* issue on the politics of separation, vol. 3 no. 1 (January 1973), p. 21.
7. A Parti Québécois pamphlet provides a short sketch of independence organizations since the start of the Quiet Revolution: Lionel Bellavance, *Les Partis Indépendantistes Québécois (1960-1970)*, Parti Québécois-Arthabaska.
8. Hubert Bauch, *Globe and Mail*, 8 September 1973.
9. See Claude Ryan's analysis in *Le Devoir*, 31 October 1973.
10. This fact is not lost on New Democrats. Tommy Douglas himself made the same point in an interview prior to the October 1973 election. See *Le Devoir*, 13 October 1973. And British Columbia's David Barrett talked seriously after the election about the possibility of linking the NDP and PQ in some fashion.
11. See, for example, the report in the *Globe and Mail*, 29 September 1973.

9.   Quebec and the Right to National Self-Determination

The issue of Quebec's right to self-determination is quite frequently raised, but less often discussed. In political debate Canadians are inclined to assert as self-evident the existence or non-existence of such a right, but a good deal less inclined to subject the matter to careful analysis and assessment and to uncover the implications of the various opinions. Supporting argument, whichever case is being advanced, tends to be assumed, rather than expressed.

Whatever one's ultimate conclusion about the right of self-determination might be, the fact that there has at no time been any sustained consideration of it may be regarded as unfortunate by all who believe that there is a clear and continuing possibility of the country breaking up. This is so because a discussion of the right of self-determination inevitably focuses attention upon the respective interests and attitudes of French and English Canada as distinct communities and upon the posture each might legitimately assume with respect to the other in the event of a declared intention of secession.

There have been a few occasions when the question of self-determination emerged in public discussion, although they have been infrequent. We mentioned in the previous chapter the case of the truncated debate within the New Democratic Party in 1971 in which the Waffle group and the Quebec provincial branch of the party called upon the NDP (and ultimately the Canadian people as a whole) to recognize Quebec's absolute right to self-determination.

Abraham Rotstein picked up the theme in the March 1971 issue of *Canadian Forum* and argued that the critical feature of this position might be the fact that English Canada formally recognized Quebec's right to determine its own future, for this would provide a symbolic separation and fresh start for the two communities and would perhaps exorcise at last the ghost of 1759. Thus the extension to Quebec of the absolute right to self-determination might be the very thing which would ensure that it will never be exercised. This is a peculiar and peculiarly Canadian argument, as Rotstein himself realized. Most independence movements, for example, assert the right, not as a means of wresting symbolic concessions from the other side, but as a device to smooth the pathway to sovereignty and to accelerate the pace of change. In the context of Quebec society as a whole, it is conceivable that a symbolic gesture of this sort might be of some marginal significance, although the reality for which the symbol presumably stands is surely what will count in the crunch. If we have the symbol without the corresponding open-mindedness and willingness to consider fundamental political change, we shall not have improved our situation; and if we have the latter, I suspect we can get along very well without the former.

As we mentioned earlier, the special Joint Committee of the Senate and the House of Commons on the Constitution, which produced its *Final Report* in 1972, included a chapter dealing with the question of self-determination. There is some useful supporting argument in the chapter, but the position of the committee is summarized in the two relevant recommendations:

> 6. The preamble of the Constitution should recognize that the Canadian federation is based on the liberty of the person and the protection of basic human rights as a fundamental and essential purpose of the State. Consequently, the preamble should also recognize that the existence of Canadian society rests on the free consent of its citizens and their collective will to live together, and that any differences among them should be settled by peaceful means.

> 7. If the citizens of a part of Canada at some time democratically declared themselves in favour of political arrangements which were contrary to the continuation of our present political structures, the disagreement should be resolved by political negotiation, not by the use of military or other coercive force.

What the committee was seeking to do, as it made clear in its explanation of the recommendations, was to map out a position which will permit the rejection of the logic and rhetoric of nationalism, and yet make possible a peaceful resolution of a secessionist crisis, should such a crisis at some point arise. It did this by lodging the right of self-determination in the individual rather than in the nation or the state, and by starting from the firm assumption that the liberty of the person and the protection of human rights is "a fundamental and essential purpose of the State" (*the* fundamental purpose, in the French-language version). From this the committee argued that the employment of force by the state to keep a section of the country within Confederation when it had democratically declared its will to go was illegitimate and unacceptable, and that the conflict should be resolved by negotiation.

This seems to me to be perfectly sensible so far as it goes, and as a brief and general statement of a highly complex issue it covers the ground as well as could be expected. I would, however, enter two *caveats*. First, the compatibility of the rights of the individual and the rights of the collectivity is asserted, rather than explained and, since the case rests on the interconnection between these two notions, fuller explication would seem to be called for. One of the continuing problems of democratic theory is the reconciliation of democracy as a form of government with the rights of minorities and individuals. Secondly, the case for including clauses relating to the possible disintegration of the country within the revised constitution has not perhaps been satisfactorily established. While the committee's formulation of the approach to a secessionist crisis has much to recommend it, inclusion of statements such as those quoted above as clauses within the constitution may impose rigidities on the situation and create difficulties which could have been avoided if the conflict were left more open to the workings of the political process. It should be remembered, however, that the committee was suffering from considerable internal stress, and this may account in part for the particular form which the recommendations took and, indeed, for their inclusion in the *Report*.

The publication of the *Final Report* occasioned dissenting

statements from a number of the committee members, the most important of which was that of two Quebec MPs, Pierre de Bané (Liberal) and Martial Asselin (Progressive Conservative). Their statement objected to the *Final Report* on the grounds that it did not deal in any adequate way with the central issue in constitutional reform: the position of Quebec in the Canadian federal system.[1] The two authors argued forcefully that Quebec's difficulties were "the result of basic contradictions between Canada's political and sociological reality and her legal and institutional system," and asserted the view that much more drastic measures than those which were contained in the *Report* must be implemented if the growing tension in Canadian political affairs were to be resolved. De Bané and Asselin made three specific constitutional recommendations: first, that the preamble of the constitution should include explicit recognition of the existence and aspirations of Quebec society; second that within the body of the constitution itself Quebec society, and hence Quebec, be accorded a basic right to self-determination; and third, that the central government be shorn of its residual powers and that it have jurisdiction only over those areas which are expressly assigned to it.

We are of course particularly interested in the second recommendation, and the authors advanced two arguments in support of it. First, it is possible that Quebec may opt for independence at some point in the future, and the inclusion of a right to self-determination in the constitution is likely to encourage a rational and orderly resolution of the problem. Secondly, because the dissatisfaction in Quebec is due in part to certain psychological causes, it could be (à la Rotstein) that "if Quebec did have the right to self-determination, it might not make use of it for the very reason that it knew this option existed." However, it seems to me that these arguments are drastically weakened by the fact that the enunciation of such an extraordinary right in a constitution must inevitably be done in abstract and general terms, whereas circumstances and detail count for everything in its application. Also, as in the case of the Rotstein argument, the assertion of the principle is likely to be of little benefit, and may even be harmful, unless the meaning and implications of the principle are well understood by Canadians and there is a general willingness to permit it to be applied in a concrete situation. There is very little evidence to suggest that English Canada at the moment is prepared to see a radical change in the position of Quebec *within* Confederation, and I therefore fail to see how one can expect there to be much readiness to accept a province's right to *leave* Confederation. The question of theoretical adequacy aside, what is the point of asserting a right if the conditions which are essential to its exercise do not exist?

What do people mean when they speak of Quebec possessing a right of self-determination? In one sense, they are suggesting that with respect to the most fundamental decisions a community is likely to make, Quebec should be regarded as if it were *already* independent and possessed of sovereign power. Quebec is conceptually set apart and distinguished from the country as a whole, and it is argued that so far as the principles of its internal organization and its relationship to the rest of the country are concerned, it ought to be the sole judge and final arbiter of what this organization and these relationships shall be. Quebec may decide to continue its membership in Confederation or it may not, but that is something for the Québécois themselves to decide, as and when they see fit. Federalism is rather like a voluntary association in which one can take out or turn in one's membership.

When the right of self-determination is analysed in this way, it can be seen that it has already departed a fair distance from reality, for it makes no sense to suggest that Quebec will negotiate with the federal government (as it does) about medicare and taxation and family allowances, and that it will abide by authoritative rulings of a single Supreme Court, but that when it comes to the question of secession it may justifiably exercise a right unilaterally to make its own independent decision. And yet what else can be meant by the assertion of the right, especially in the case of those (such as the NDP-Quebec, the Waffle and Abraham Rotstein) who speak of Quebec's *absolute* right to self-determination? Why absolute? And, anyway, what *is* an absolute right?

One might perhaps prefer at this point to scale down the claim considerably, and point out that there is a danger of treating the passion-filled terms of politics as if they were philosophical statements. Thus the practical message in such a claim, it may be said, is tolerably clear; in plain language what most people really mean when they employ this high-flown talk of absolute rights is that if Quebec decides it wants to get out, then the rest of Canada shouldn't fight to keep it in. Assuming that it is possible to specify satisfactorily what would constitute a "decision" by Quebec to depart and what would compose a fair separation settlement, this seems to me to be eminently sensible and will, I hope, prove to be the ultimate view of those Canadians who think about such matters.

However, this simple and reasonable position is unnecessarily puffed up by the appeal to an absolute right of self-determination, and this at the price of considerable intellectual confusion and the gratuitous creation of opposition in circles where there need be little or none. There is as well a more practical danger; to approach the issue on the assumption that it involves the *rights* rather than or more than the *interests* of the two communities is very likely to produce a set of attitudes on each side which will exacerbate rather than help to resolve the conflict, and when the issue touches people's lives in the way that secession does, this is no small matter. Interests may legitimately be the subject of bargaining and adjustment, whereas rights are expressed or asserted or claimed —no one except Faust bargains with his rights.

One need not look far to find the reason for such rhetorical inflation. Since the eighteenth century there has been an ever-increasing reluctance to speak of expedience, however broadly and humanely defined, and in consequence an elaborate vocabulary has arisen to assist people in the task of disguising their thoughts from themselves. The British philosopher, J. D. Mabbott, gives a graphic indication of the modern tendency to employ the doctrine of natural rights at every opportunity: "Six months' scrutiny of a correspondence column revealed a natural right to a living wage, a right to work, a right to trial by jury, a right to buy cigarettes after 8 p.m., a right to camp in a caravan by the roadside, and a right to walk on the grouse moors of Scotland during the close season."[2]

At the international level, the sudden rise and the great

strength of nationalism and the widespread appeal of the politics of national liberation has been one of the major factors introducing the language of moral absolutes into the mundane affairs of state. In many circumstances the concept of the rights of nations supplanted that of raison d'état, and was able to get a powerful purchase on men's minds and awaken a sympathy in their hearts. We have seen in an earlier chapter the animus of Wilsonian liberal nationalism against the tawdry demands of national self-interest, but we have had occasion to note as well the difficulties into which Wilson's brand of international morality led him and many of those with whom he came in contact. Canadians, it may be pointed out, who have disengaged themselves from one sphere of influence only to find they have unwittingly backed into another, are veritable specialists in avoiding unpleasant talk of national interest; indeed, Canada's fate has always been viewed within the context of a larger political and economic system. French Canadians, because their situation has been more sharply defined, have customarily evinced a more lively collective sense of the interests of their community than have their fellow citizens. This disparity continues today and presents an alarming prospect for English Canadians who see French Canada defining itself more and more autonomously, without a strong reciprocating movement emerging in the rest of the country directed towards defining or redefining the character and purposes of English Canada.

I can think of three, and perhaps four, ways in which an attempt might be made to establish the existence of Quebec's right to self-determination, and on balance none of them is satisfactory. The first, which we can dispose of quickly, is the argument that there is some provision in the positive law of the Canadian state which recognizes the right of component parts of the federation to secede. This, it is widely recognized, is simply not true. Canada, like many countries, recognizes the right of individuals to resign membership and to emigrate with their possessions, but there is nothing to be found in the British North America Act or related legislation which provides for a single province's unilateral decision to secede from the federation. Indeed, there are no explicit, stipulated procedures allowing for a collective decision by the eleven constituent governments together to terminate the federal experiment, although there are clearly ways in which this might in fact be done, perhaps via the existing arrangements for constitutional amendment.

It would appear that in terms of existing constitutional principles any legitimate secession on the part of one of the provinces would be effected by the normal procedures for constitutional amendment, which is to say, a Joint Address of the Canadian Parliament to the United Kingdom Parliament. The British Parliament would be involved in this process because the Canadian provinces and federal government have never been able to agree on a domestic amending procedure and so the ultimate although admittedly *pro forma* constitutional authority would lie with Great Britain.

It is unlikely in the extreme that Britain would intervene directly in such a matter, and still more unlikely that it would be prepared to deal directly with the seceding province. Just because it is a *pro forma* authority, the obvious posture for Great Britain to adopt would be one of non-interference, and it could best accomplish this by maintaining its traditional role in Canadian constitutional affairs. Thus in matters affecting the constitution it is to be expected that Britain would listen to the federal government and be deaf to the provinces.

There are a variety of precedents relating to secession, some of them conflicting, which have arisen out of Great Britain's relations with its colonial or ex-colonial territories.[3] The one which almost certainly would be taken to apply here is the case of the state of Western Australia in the 1930s. As a result of growing dissatisfaction within that state about its membership in the Australian federation, a referendum was held at which secession was approved. The state government then sent a petition directly to the British Parliament requesting that it pass legislation dissolving Western Australia's ties to Australia as a whole. The British Parliament refused to receive the petition on the grounds that it did not have the support of the federal government. A generally similar position was taken up with respect to Penang in Malaya in 1951 and Western Nigeria in 1954.

Although there are conflicting precedents, it is reasonable to argue that these do not apply to Canada. An instance of quite different behaviour on the part of the British government may be found in the break-up of the West Indies Federation; there Britain permitted Jamaica to secede without prior consultation with the federal government. But apart from the fact that Jamaica was by far the most influential member of the federation, with the largest territory, more than half the federal population and almost half the revenue, the West Indies Federation was a new political organization. In fact it was formed in 1958 and dissolved in 1962. One will find that the conflcting cases are almost invariably those in which the participants have had only a brief and often turbulent experience with federal government. Consider, for example, not just the West Indies Federation, but the partition of India in 1947, the post-referendum separation of the Southern Cameroons in 1961, and the granting of separate independence to Zambia and Malawi in 1962—all of which Britain accepted.

If the argument from positive law, from the constitution of the country, is of no use in establishing a right to self-determination, one might fall back on the second alternative, which is to ground Quebec's right in principles which are taken to be superior to the positive law of any particular state, to appeal, for example, to natural law. The idea of a law of nature has had a long and colourful tradition, but there are limits beyond which even this most pliant and serviceable of principles cannot be made to stretch. It has traditionally served as a transcendent, non-political criterion for assessing the actions of rulers and subjects. In Roman and medieval times it was indeed often related to another concept, the *jus gentium* or law of nations, which was employed to assist in the regulation of relations between communities with distinct cultures and backgrounds. But this latter was mainly a conservative principle which was used to smooth out relations between human groups, not to justify political secession. That sort of thing never went down well in the Roman Empire. In the modern period the concept of natural law has been utilized to explain the proper relationship between the individual and the state and between the individual and his fellow man. In this way of thinking, as we have suggested above, the basic unit of analysis and the natural entity which political activity benefits is the individual person, not an aggregate of persons such as the state, the nation, or a social class. Unless one were to suppose that a universal, natural duty obliging states to recognize the right of component parts to dissolve the bonds tying them to the larger structure is part of a system of natural law, it is difficult to imagine how the concept of a law of nature can be of much service in establishing Quebec's right unilaterally to determine its own future.

A third alternative, and no doubt the one that most advocates have in mind, is to rest Quebec's case squarely on the right of nations to lead an independent existence if they so choose. Although this apparently straightforward nationalist argument has been prevalent for more than a century, we have seen in earlier chapters that it nevertheless contains a nest of difficulties. To re-cap briefly, in order to speak of a group of people possessing a collective right, it is first necessary to invest that collectivity with some corporate identity. The members of an audience at a pop festival or the fans at a hockey game do not as a body possess rights, whereas the members of a trade union or service club do; the important difference between these groups lies in this corporate dimension. There is no difficulty in appreciating how such juridically defined units as states and business corporations may be understood to have rights and duties, but such associations are the product of human decision and identifiable acts of recognition. A nation, however, does not derive its identity from recognition, for it is deemed to be a natural unit. The point of the nationalist argument is that a nation is not the creation of a political order (as is a business corporation, for example), but is itself the creator of a political order; where a nation exists, so should a state. A nation is prior to the state in the same sense that individuals are, and it enjoys the right to form a state for itself. Where does his right come from? A nationalist will invest rights in the nation by following a process which is rather similar to that of an individualist when he lodges rights and duties in the human individual. One views the individual, the other the nation, as the political ultimate.

However, unlike the individualist, the nationalist faces a thorny problem of definition, for nationhood is a much more elusive identity than human personality. No one could declare that he is unable to "see" individuals without awakening suspicions about his sanity, but it is perfectly possible for someone to say that he cannot perceive nations in the sense that the nationalist intends without his being thought soft in the head. To provide straight nationalist grounds for Quebec's right to self-determination noticeably alters the basis of the whole argument, for whatever realistic set of indicators might be used for identifying the "Quebec nation," the result would certainly not be simply to identify the nation with the existing population and territory of the province of Quebec. The French-Canadian nation would obviously exclude some of the people living in Quebec and include some of the people (and some of the territory?) beyond its borders. If there were to be a referendum on secession, within the terms of the nationalist argument why shouldn't the French-Canadian communities in the Ontario counties bordering Quebec be included as well as the Acadian population of New Brunswick? Why, on the other hand, shouldn't the English-language communities on the Quebec side of the Ottawa River be given the separate opportunity to declare with which group they choose to associate? For obvious reasons, people choose not to put this sort of argument forward directly, preferring to detect a happy but fictional coincidence between the province of Quebec and the French-Canadian nation.

Given the problems of definition and implementation, then, a pure nationalist argument for the right to self-determination either will not work properly, or else it works too well. Either it has to be manhandled and quite seriously twisted out of shape in order to be made to fit the actual circumstances, or else it places in the hands of any substantial and coherent cultural minorities who care to wield it a potent weapon and a justification for minority self-determination which, on principle, it will be very difficult for the newly independent nation to resist. Such an argument seems to be neither theoretically satisfactory, nor practically tenable in Canadian circumstances.

Nevertheless, we have seen in an earlier chapter that the

doctrine of self-determination has been asserted with great frequency in modern times and, although its status in international law and relations is still very unclear, it has in this century gained fairly wide acceptance. However, the important thing from our point of view is that, even if it could be conclusively established that the right to self-determination is a valid principle of international law, it would nevertheless have to be recognized that Quebec does not fall into the category of cases to which that right would then apply. And so an appeal to the principles of international law fails on two grounds: first, self-determination has not as yet been conclusively established as an international legal right; and second, the principle of self-determination, which has developed primarily in connection with European decolonization, does not at present apply to a case such as that of Quebec or French Canada.

Although an attempt might be made to extend that right by analogy to "national" groups wishing to secede from the political communities to which their members belong, it seems clear that this is not as yet an accepted construction of the right to self-determination. Given the vexing ambiguity of nationalist concepts, it is no wonder that international lawyers, who exercise a Burkean circumspection in these matters, have been reluctant to venture into that "great Serbonian bog, betwixt Damiata and Mount Casius old, where armies whole have sunk."

This leaves us, then, with the fourth and final alternative which might be called the Hobbesian hypothesis, after the seventeenth-century political philosopher who presented this argument in its most convincing form. Viewing the maintenance of life and limb as the first and foremost goal of men, Hobbes argued that men have an absolute right to preserve themselves; that is to say, a man can justifiably do anything to save himself if his life is in danger. One can see that this reasoning might be readily transferred to a province or nation which believes its existence is threatened, and, indeed, Hobbes himself actually applied the same sort of analysis to the field of international relations, arguing that states have an absolute right to act in any way they deem necessary to preserve themselves.

Apart from the fact that Hobbes explicitly denied the exercise of this right to all subordinate entities in a state so long as there was a sovereign effectively maintaining the peace, this line of reasoning founders as soon as one appreciates the idiosyncratic way in which Hobbes uses the term "right." Neither the natural right of individuals nor the parallel right of sovereign states entails duties; that is to say, there is no duty laid upon any given individual or state to respect the natural right of others, nor is there any duty laid upon the others to respect the rights of the given individual or state. The right of each individual and of each state is not limited by the requirement of respecting the rights of others. *Absolute* natural rights are not logically speaking part and parcel of a moral order, but the symbol of the absence of a moral order. Therefore, if Quebec is considered to have this kind of right, it does not follow that the rest of Canada has a duty to respect it.

It should be apparent now that those Canadians who speak of Quebec's absolute right to self-determination, if their words are taken literally, have left the world of moral discourse behind them. For they are saying that Quebec, unilaterally and without regard to the rest of the country, must possess the freedom to organize its affairs as it sees fit, and that the rest of the country has an unlimited obligation to stand aside while Quebec does this. The logical weakness of this position, as we have seen, is that conditions are enunciated in which right is entirely on one side and duty entirely on the other, which means in fact that there is neither right nor duty. The practical difficulty is that one is not speaking of two communities which are already sovereign and distinct from one another, but of a single country which is to be broken apart, and it is absurd to think that the group which is proposing to secede should or could be permitted unilaterally to dictate the conditions of secession on the understanding that the other group would be committed willy-nilly to accept and respect them. *Real politik* is preferable to this kind of absolutist morality.

I would argue, then, that the claim that Quebec possesses a right to self-determination is either mistaken or else it is a misleading and unfortunate way of saying something worthwhile and important: namely, that the values of civility to which

Canadians aspire, and which they sometimes achieve, preclude the application of force to stop a secessionist movement of the kind contemplated, and that civilized values are in this case backed up by plain ordinary self-interest, since the group in question is large enough to knock the whole political system off its foundations if its settled desires go unrecognized for too long.

Edmund Burke is no doubt *persona non grata* with some of the people who assert Quebec's absolute right to self-determination, but he nevertheless displayed a wonderful capacity to talk sense, and he was clearly on the "right" side in the American struggle for independence in the eighteenth century. He refused to discuss the issues involved in that controversy in terms of abstract rights. "It is not," he writes in his *Speech on Conciliation with America,* "what a lawyer tells me I *may* do; but what humanity, reason and justice tell me I ought to do. Is a politic act the worse for being a generous one? Is no concession proper, but that which is made from your want of right to keep what you grant? Or does it lessen the grace or dignity of relaxing in the exercise of an odious claim, because you have your evidence-room full of titles, and your magazines stuffed with arms to enforce them? What signify all those titles, and all those arms? Of what avail are they, when the reason of the thing tells me, that the assertion of my title is the loss of my suit; and that I could do nothing but wound myself by the use of my own weapons?"[4]

Burke's lesson is as timely today as when he wrote, and it is instructive to note that his argument was directed against the dogmatic assertion of right in Great Britain, not in America. The moral is applicable to both sides of the controversy. Where there is basic conflict between two segments of a political community, argument about absolute rights is of little help. It is misleading. It engenders needless opposition (and perhaps the wrong kind of support). And it encourages the development of hardened positions which are relatively impermeable to negotiation, rather than a spirit of toleration, or at least a willingness to recognize limits beyond which action will be mutually destructive. If either side construes the issue as one of "national honour," "absolute rights" and "the integrity of the state," then the outlook will be bleak indeed; if, on the other hand, it is viewed less dramatically as a conflict about the institutional arrangements appropriate to the two communities, there is at least the possibility that if we have to take the trip we shall all arrive at our destination (whatever it may be) uninjured, and—who knows?—perhaps even the better for our journey.

NOTES

1. It was published in the May 1972 issue of the *Canadian Forum*.
2. *The State and the Citizen* (London: Arrow Books, 1958), p. 58.
3. R. L. Watts' article in R. M. Burns, ed., *One Country or Two?* is useful here, and I am indebted to it.
4. *The Works of Edmund Burke*, vol. I, p. 479.

10.   Love of One's Own
and Love of the Good

Edmund Burke's sophisticated and sympathetic reaction to the
problems of Britain's American colonies indicates that the issue
of secession can be comprehended within perspectives other
than that of nationalism and the right of self-determination. If
the nationalist argument is inadequate, as we have suggested,
the question arises as to what principled position an English
Canadian might appropriately assume when confronted with a
strong independence movement in Quebec and the possibility
of an eventual attempt at secession.

There is a way in which English Canada can approach this
issue sensibly and humanely, and its general outline has become
clear in the course of our study of nationalism and liberty in
the previous chapters. What is needed is an understanding of
the problem which permits one to reject the claim of a right to
national self-determination and to avoid fanning the flames of
nationalism in Quebec, without at the same time necessitating
the adoption of a rigidly anti-nationalist position which would
run the risk of being turned into an anti-democratic position if
a secessionist crisis actually occurred. A commitment to democratic and libertarian principles rules out, or so it seems to me,
the employment of force by the state to keep a section of the
country such as Quebec within Confederation when it has freely
and clearly declared its will to go. It would be difficult for
someone who values democratic government and respect for
persons to justify the exercise of the powers of the state to
thwart or block the settled convictions of a large and terri-
torially coherent segment of the political community.

We have had occasion to note, however, that principles which
are clear enough in the abstract have a way of becoming complicated and confused when they appear in the political arena.
Even such an apparently straightforward matter as determining

who are the "people" whose future is at issue can be a contentious and complex business. Consider the case of the seceding southern states in the American Civil War. From the point of view of democratic principles, an assessment of the position of the southern states is complicated by the fact that they were bent on continuing to deny their black populations basic human rights. An appeal to the legitimacy of decisions made by the "people" according to the constitutions of the several states was bound to be unconvincing, since so far as the slave question was concerned it was the adequacy of the definition of the citizen body and the actual legitimacy of the constitutional principles themselves that were the primary issue.

A contemporary situation which is similar in this respect is the still unresolved conflict between Great Britain and Rhodesia. It is clear that a large majority of Rhodesian citizens as defined by the constitution were in favour of Premier Ian Smith's unilateral declaration of independence from Britain in 1965, and continue to support the *de facto* independence which has never received *de jure* recognition by Great Britain or the United Nations. But the unreality in this expression of collective will, and the reason why the outside world refuses to recognize the legitimacy of the Rhodesian regime, is to be found in the fact that the constitutional system entrenches white-settler minority rule and condemns the majority black population to continued denial of political power and civil rights. In such circumstances, it would be folly to expect that decisions issuing out of the normal constitutional and political process in any way reflect the will or advance the interests of the society as a whole. Acceptance of the adequacy of contemporary Rhodesian constitutional arrangements would mean the abandonment of the bulk of the community to an indefinite period of exploitation and suppression.

These are admittedly extreme cases, but they do serve to illustrate the difficulties that can be encountered in attempting to reconcile principles with the complexities of practice. In this light it is clear that the implications of the position we are defending, namely, the renunciation of force to prevent secession, have to be drawn out in some detail. For all practical purposes, the unit within Canada which might realistically be the forum for the expression of secessionist sentiments is the province, and, as we have seen, the only province in the federal system which is currently capable of mounting a serious challenge is Quebec. Hypothetically, one might conceive of Alberta, metropolitan Toronto or Newfoundland as possible secessionist units, but this at the moment is to enter the world of make-believe. However, the challenge from Quebec is credible, and its provincial political structures are sufficiently sophisticated and autonomous to provide an institutional channel for the expression of a collective decision.

While the application of force to stop Quebec from leaving Confederation seems to me to be illegitimate and something to be strenuously resisted, it is necessary to state that this does not by any means exhaust the range of possibilities within which the use of force might have to be contemplated.

We have discussed earlier the difficulties which are encountered in securing the free and sober expression of opinion of a community. Most of the time conventional arrangements and rough-and-ready methods are relied upon to permit an approximate voicing of the opinion of a society; it is apparent that the difficulties encountered in achieving such an expression in the midst of a political crisis are markedly exacerbated, particularly when it is a question of settling one of the most fundamental choices which a group of people can make.

What at bottom is at issue here are the limitations and the vulnerability of the democratic process as it operates in modern states, a process which seems quite well-suited to handle some matters, and ill-equipped to cope with others. The normal public business of a community can be conducted within the framework of the conventional arrangements and express the goals of the society tolerably well. However, when extraordinary and extraordinarily divisive decisions have to be taken, it is often discovered that the substructure of common assumptions and good will has crumbled and will no longer adequately support the institutions through which the conflict must be channelled. Citizens elsewhere in Canada have in my view an important and legitimate interest in the health of democratic institutions in Quebec (and vice versa), particularly when the consequences of provincial policy will affect them so directly. The federal government for its part has a constitutional obligation to maintain peace, order and good government in the country, but it has as well a more general responsibility for supporting the democratic process within the province and for helping to bring about the humane and orderly settlement of the nationalist crisis by the country as a whole. One cannot sensibly be blind to the possibility that, in circumstances of widespread intimidation and the threat of disorder, the responsibilities of the federal government might require the employment of force to guarantee or re-establish the democratic process.

Having said this, it is important to indicate the circumstances in which the powers of the state might appropriately be used in this way and to emphasize the real dangers of their misuse. Even with the best will in the world, government officials, faced with a rapidly developing crisis, might be unable to be as attentive to the distinction between legitimate and illegitimate political opposition and militance as they would wish to be; and given the fact that the interests of one or a number of the parties to the conflict might be significantly advanced by the neglect or none too scrupulous recognition of this distinction, the temptations of obscurity and confusion might be well-nigh irresistible. It has been persuasively argued that in the October Crisis of 1970 neither the government of Quebec nor the federal government was careful to respect the difference between militant but legitimate opposition and terrorism, and to ensure that the steps which they took and the statements which they made would clarify rather than obscure the differences in the minds of the public.[1]

There is no denying that the task of the federal government in confronting the issue of Quebec secession would be extraordinarily difficult. In large measure this is because it would be constrained to play two distinct and often conflicting roles. On the one hand, it would have to act as a kind of umpire-cum-police officer, containing and regulating the political forces at work so that the resolution of the conflict could be conducted in a peaceful and orderly fashion. On the other hand, it would have inevitably to act as the spokesman of English Canada, and in that capacity to protect and advance the interests of that part of the country. The requirements of objectivity and advocacy sit uneasily together and would impose terrible tensions on the central government, and yet it does not seem to me that there is any practicable way in which this could be avoided. Given the history of the country and the shape of politics in Canada, it is to the institutions of the federal government that the rest of the country would have ultimately to look for representation of its interests and point of view in any conflict with Quebec. The other provinces would clearly have a profound interest in the way in which the issue was resolved and a great deal at stake in any final settlement, and one would anticipate that the central government would be subjected to intense (and often conflicting pressures) from this source. However, unless the crisis precipitated the collapse rather than the constitution of any common purpose, the federal government and legislature would be looked to as Canada's spokesman if for no other reason than that it is the only possible institutional focus of authority to which Canadians in the circumstances could turn.

In its role as an umpire, it would seem to me that the federal government would possess the right to declare that it sees itself as having an obligation to ensure that any decision which is taken as to the future constitutional status of Quebec is a genuine expression of the will of the community and to ensure that the minimum institutional requirements for the expression are met. Thus, for example, it could appropriately insist that a referendum be held in Quebec specifically on the question of the province's future and under the joint supervision of the federal and provincial governments. It would then have the related responsibility (again, shared with the provincial authorities) of ensuring that the expression of opinion was as free as possible and not subject to coercion or intimidation.

All of this is based on the prior acceptance of the view that the question of separation is a legitimate if extraordinary political issue which must be met fairly and openly and resolved according to democratic procedures. If this is to mean anything, it must signify that all sides recognize that Quebec might properly initiate negotiations with the central government which could in principle lead to the province's accession to sovereign independence. There are obviously a variety of other possible conclusions to such discussions, but this perspective does commit all participants to abstain from setting out rigid limits in advance and to conduct negotiations in good faith.

This by no means entails the suspension by the various parties of concern about their own interests. Quite the reverse; what it does is provide a framework of common assumptions within which the interests and goals of the two communities can be expressed and their conflicts settled. Some underlying accord, even if it is only procedural, is necessary if bargaining and negotiation is to proceed, and it is this which the firm location of secession within the realm of legitimate politics could be expected to provide. Generally speaking, the bargaining position of English Canada would be strong and, if it came to the question of separation, her main objectives would no doubt be reasonably clear. She would want the equitable division of public assets and liabilities; the protection of English-language minorities in Quebec; beneficial economic relationships with the new state and the fair treatment of existing English-Canadian business interests in Quebec; and guaranteed lines of communication between the Maritimes and the rest of Canada, together with the unfettered use of the Seaway system. There may well be other matters to add to this list, but these would certainly be central issues about which English Canada would be seeking satisfaction. Quebec, of course, would have its own list, and one would hope that it would be during the complicated process of negotiation that the concrete achievement of secession would be accomplished, rather than in a dramatic, but primarily symbolic unilateral declaration of independence.

This story of nationalism has raised some broad questions relating to culture and nationality which we are able here only to touch on by way of conclusion. For example, our consideration of the relationship between individual and social freedom has forced us to take notice of the vital significance of cultural affiliations in constituting personal identity. A person's conception of who he is and what it is important for him to do is in significant measure the product of the culture to which he belongs. Montesquieu expressed the interrelationship between personality and community in an aphorism about political leadership: "at the birth of societies, it is the leaders of the republic who shape the institutions, but afterwards it is the institutions which shape the leaders of the republic." The cultural matrix within which liberty is exercised may be as important as the liberty itself in determining the course of human affairs.

A recognition of the constitutive power of culture and of the dependence of individuals in the modern world on large and complex associations lies beneath most expressions of nationalist sentiment. Notwithstanding the important findings of social scientists that nationalism is often an instrument of social change and that it frequently works to the benefit of the economically powerful classes in society, it remains true that a major source of the widespread appeal and the potency of the doctrine is the gnawing concern about the loss of communal (and therefore, to a fair extent, personal) identity and the worry about excessive dependence on what are perceived to be external forces.

George Grant's formulation of the importance of culture for autonomy and creation is eloquent and concise: "In human life there must always be place for love of the good and love of one's own. Love of the good is man's highest end, but it is of the nature of things that we come to know and to love what is good by first meeting it in that which is our own—this particular body, this family, these friends, this woman, this part of the world, this set of traditions, this country, this civilization."[2] We begin life with a direct experience of particular things, with the immediacy of the here and now, and grow towards a conception of what is right and fitting from an initial sense of what is familiar. The purposes which we believe we should serve and the ways in which we conceive and exercise our freedom arise, not as an unbought gift of grace, but issue rather out of what we have been and what we are becoming. Small wonder that banishment was among the most severe of punishments in the city-states of ancient Greece. A man without a homeland, an *homme déraciné*, suffers a double deprivation. He is deprived because he lacks the comfort of familiar things and the informal affirmation of his identity which he sees in his surroundings; and he is deprived because the roots which nourish and support his life's quest are cut, and the vitalizing interplay between character and circumstance, habit and reason, experience and purpose, is interrupted. It can be a painful and a lengthy process to connect these things up again.

It is Grant's conviction that Canada has long since lost whatever possibility it may once have had of nurturing a distinctively Canadian sense of one's own, that "Canada" is now a term which denotes a country that might have been, but which failed. *Lament for a Nation*, which he published in 1965, sang the swan song for Canada; since that time, appropriately enough, Canada as a significant category of analysis has pretty well disappeared from view altogether in his work. As Grant says in the preface to *Technology and Empire*, a collection of papers published in 1969, the essays there included are "all perspectives on what it is to live in the Great Lakes region of North America"; the border between the two countries is as nothing compared to the unity of culture and aspiration which binds together the industrial heartland of the continent. Thus, whatever traditions buttress and animate our pursuit of the good, they are assuredly not Canadian at the root. Grant sees America as the prime carrier of the culture of liberalism, a doctrine and a mode of living which glories in modernity and innovation, and is profoundly hostile to traditional cultures of continuity and enjoyment; and he sees Canada as a derivative participant in the American experience. Their own is our own, and their good, ours.

George Grant's fatalistic judgment about his country relates very much to Canada as a whole, and the failure which he records is the failure of Canadians to create for themselves a single, coherent national community on the northern half of the continent which was able to stand against the pressures of American liberalism because it stood for something distinctive. Although much more radical in his analysis, Grant is in one of the dominant traditions of English-Canadian nationalist thought, a tradition which emphasizes the crucial role of the central government and the crown in constituting a nation out of diverse regions and peoples and investing it with a distinctive character and a sense of purpose. •

However, other people have held other conceptions of

Canada and Canadian society, conceptions which in some cases possess at least the modest advantage of not committing the adherent immediately to political quietism and which may in fact build on a firmer acceptance of contemporary reality. Northrop Frye begins from a position which appears to be rather similar to that of Grant when he comments on Canada's "lack of will to resist its own disintegration," and argues that "it is practically the only country left in the world which is a pure colony, colonial in psychology as well as in mercantile economics."[3] But Frye in the same passage gives an important reason other than the pervasive influence of American liberalism for why this should be so, and in so doing challenges a major assumption in Grant's argument. What Frye adds in essence is the fact of cultural pluralism, and he does this by distinguishing between the ideas of unity and identity in Canadian life: "identity is local and regional, rooted in the imagination and in works of culture; unity is national in reference, international in perspective, and rooted in a political feeling." Frye does not deny that certain minimal elements of a national identity exist, but he does insist that most of the characteristic cultural and imaginative factors common to the country as a whole, such as the brutality of the climate, have functioned as negative influences.

Frye is surely correct in arguing that identity in Canada has been primarily a regional thing, involving the sense of belonging which people have felt for their own locality; national unity, however grand in aspiration, has in fact been formal in character, something to be discovered primarily in the complex and always temporary reconciliation of the interests of the diverse groups and regions which compose the country. Federalism in Canada has not been just a political structure, but a stark sociological fact as well. The difficulties experienced in sustaining diversity in the maelstrom of change and homogenization which has characterized the modern world are awesome. Indeed, a cynic might describe Canada as a collection of regions which have been subjected to roughly equivalent doses of Americanization, and there would be an element of truth in this assertion. In any case, Canadians have found it necessary to attempt to chart an uneasy course between asserting or imposing an artificial, pan-Canadian solidarity on the one hand, and courting disintegration on the other. Frye puts it this way: "The tension between this political sense of unity and the imaginative sense of locality is the essence of whatever the word 'Canadian' means. Once the tension is given up, and the two elements of unity and identity are confused or assimilated to each other, we get the two endemic diseases of Canadian life. Assimilating identity to unity produces the empty gestures of cultural nationalism; assimilating unity to identity produces the kind of provincial isolation which is now called separatism."

Canadians have spent many years and much effort attempting to face up to the radical and in many ways disturbing implications of this union of diversity that they are seeking to fashion. There has been over the past decade a dawning recognition at least of the problems in the relations between French-speaking and English-speaking Canada. We are still, I suspect, very far away from a full realization of the consequences which the practical acceptance of the idea of cultural pluralism (as distinct from biculturalism) may have. And to the specifically cultural complexities with which we have been primarily concerned in this study must be added the growing tensions which mark the relationship between the federal government and those regional social and economic interests which are represented by the provinces.

What course the country will follow in the years ahead it would be foolish to attempt to predict, but one thing seems to me to be very clear. Whether one chooses to regard the Canadian historical experience as a record of folly or as a story of wisdom joining hands with virtue, there is no denying the brute fact that our past has created or permitted the emergence of a society which is shot through with diversity—cultural, economic, regional and political—and that the various forms of diversity have driven roots deep into Canadian soil. In these circumstances, it is the course of prudence, no less than of wisdom and justice, to accept and respect the various identities of which Canada is composed, to find if possible sustaining common interests to justify continued association, but to recognize if necessary the withering away of common purpose should this in the future occur.

The well-being of the state or the nation as such is not an end in itself, but a means to something else; Aristotle described that something else for all time when he stated that the end of politics and the state is the active promotion of the good life for its people. It would be tragic if the overzealous effort to keep the country together led to the neglect or distortion of one of the few fundamental opinions upon which Canadians of every description can all agree: the belief in the political supremacy of libertarian and democratic principles. If that is the price to be paid for maintaining national unity, then the price is high—far too high.

NOTES

1. See, for example, Ron Haggart and Aubrey E. Golden, *Rumours of War* (Toronto: New Press, 1971), Denis Smith, *Bleeding Hearts . . . Bleeding Country*, and for a general sampling of one section of English-Canadian opinion at the time, *The Canadian Forum*, January 1971 issue.
2. *Technology and Empire: Perspectives on North America* (Toronto: House of Anansi, 1969), p. 73.
3. *The Bush Garden: Essays on the Canadian Imagination*, Preface.

Bibliographical Note

If asked to list *the three books* which best illuminate the themes discussed in this study, I would name the following:

Elie Kedourie, *Nationalism* (London: Hutchison University Library, 1960), 145 pp.

An excellent, clear-headed but demanding examination of the emergence and fortunes of the doctrine of nationalism in Europe. Concentrates on the concept rather than on the political history of nationalism.

A. B. C. Cobban, *The Nation State and National Self-Determination* (London: Collins, 1969), 309 pp.

A rich, detailed study of the history and theory of national self-determination in Europe and elsewhere, focussing primarily on the twentieth century.

R. M. Burns, ed., *One Country or Two?* (Montreal: McGill-Queen's University Press, 1971), 287 pp.

A balanced and thoughtful collection of essays by a group of English-speaking Canadians reflecting on the question of Quebec separation and its consequences for Canada.

If asked to list *a dozen of the most useful books*, I would name, in addition to the three above, the nine which follow:

K. R. Minogue, *Nationalism* (Baltimore: Penguin Books, 1970), 168 pp.

This is a spirited account which concentrates on the history of the doctrine in nineteenth-century Europe and in the global politics of the twentieth century.

Anthony Smith, *Theories of Nationalism* (London: Duckworth, 1971), 344 pp.

This is a closely argued investigation of the various explanations which have been offered in the effort to comprehend nationalism.

P. E. Trudeau, *Federalism and the French Canadians* (Toronto: Macmillan of Canada, 1968), 212 pp.

This is an indispensable source, for the obvious reason that

169

Trudeau has been a central figure in recent Canadian public affairs, and for the less obvious reason that it is provocatively argued and explicitly related to an important intellectual tradition.

Marcel Rioux, *Quebec in Question* (Toronto: James, Lewis and Samuel, 1971), 191 pp.
An impassioned analysis of Quebec's situation by a Québécois sociologist who is committed to national independence. Chapter 7 contains a sustained critique of Trudeau's anti-nationalism.

Denis Smith, *Bleeding Hearts . . . Bleeding Country* (Edmonton: M. G. Hurtig, 1971), 177 pp.
The occasion of this study was the October Crisis of 1970, but the carefully articulated discussion of democratic and nationalist theory and its relation to practice invests the book with enduring significance.

Pierre Vallières, *White Niggers of America* (Toronto: McClelland and Stewart, 1971), 278 pp.
This is an extraordinary autobiographical and intellectual statement by a preternaturally sensitive Québécois intelligence. More significant as a kind of French-Canadian equivalent to Rousseau's *Confessions* than as an assertion of radical nationalism.

Ramsay Cook, *Canada and the French-Canadian Question* (Toronto: Macmillan of Canada, 1967), 219 pp.
This book and the one below are important collections of essays on nationalism and history in Quebec and Canada by one of the country's most distinguished English-Canadian students of Quebec.

Ramsay Cook, *The Maple Leaf Forever* (Toronto: Macmillan of Canada, 1971), 253 pp.

Ramsay Cook, ed., *French-Canadian Nationalism* (Toronto: Macmillan of Canada, 1969).
A useful anthology of work by French Canadians writing about themselves and their community.

For those who wish to pursue specific topics further, there are a number of helpful bibliographical aids on Canada and Quebec, among which I would name the following:

Jacques Cotnam, *Contemporary Quebec: An Analytical Bibliography* (Toronto: McClelland and Stewart, 1973), 111 pp.

Robert Boily, *Québec 1940–1969: Bibliographie* (Montreal: Les Presses de l'Université de Montréal, 1971), 208 pp.

Robert Fulford et al, *Read Canadian: A Book About Canadian Books* (Toronto: James Lewis and Samuel, 1972), 275 pp.

The literature on the history and theory of nationalism is voluminous and can be approached most efficiently by consulting the bibliographical notes of such authors as Kedourie, Minogue and Anthony Smith.

For further material relating to specific issues discussed in this book, consult the references in the text and footnotes for suggestions.

Index